SAN LEAND

Social Issues
in Literature

The Environment in Henry David Thoreau's *Walden*

DISCARD

Other Books in the Social Issues in Literature Series:

Abuse of Power in George Orwell's *Nineteen Eighty-Four*

American Dream/Alienation in John Steinbeck's *Of Mice and Men*

Bioethics in Aldous Huxley's *Brave New World*

Corruption in William Shakespeare's *Hamlet*

Gender in Sandra Cisneros's *The House on Mango Street*

Male/Female Roles in Ernest Hemingway's *The Sun Also Rises*

Political Issues in J.K. Rowling's Harry Potter Series

Race Relations in Alan Paton's *Cry, the Beloved Country*

Suicide in Arthur Miller's *Death of a Salesman*

War in Stephen Crane's *The Red Badge of Courage*

Women's Issues in Amy Tan's *The Joy Luck Club*

Social Issues
in Literature

The Environment in Henry David Thoreau's *Walden*

Gary Wiener, Book Editor

GREENHAVEN PRESS
A part of Gale, Cengage Learning

GALE
CENGAGE Learning

Detroit • New York • San Francisco • New Haven, Conn • Waterville, Maine • London

Christine Nasso, *Publisher*
Elizabeth Des Chenes, *Managing Editor*

© 2010 Greenhaven Press, a part of Gale, Cengage Learning

For more information, contact:
Greenhaven Press
27500 Drake Rd.
Farmington Hills, MI 48331-3535
Or you can visit our Internet site at gale.cengage.com

For product information and technology assistance, contact us at

Gale Customer Support, 1-800-877-4253
For permission to use material from this text or product, submit all requests online at www.cengage.com/permissions

Further permissions questions can be emailed to permissionrequest@cengage.com

Articles in Greenhaven Press anthologies are often edited for length to meet page requirements. In addition, original titles of these works are changed to clearly present the main thesis and to explicitly indicate the author's opinion. Every effort is made to ensure that Greenhaven Press accurately reflects the original intent of the authors. Every effort has been made to trace the owners of copyrighted material.

Cover photograph © Bettmann/Corbis.

LIBRARY OF CONGRESS CATALOGING-IN-PUBLICATION DATA

The environment in Henry David Thoreau's Walden / Gary Wiener, book editor.
    p. cm. -- (Social issues in literature)
    Includes bibliographical references and index.
    ISBN 978-0-7377-4654-9 -- ISBN 978-0-7377-4655-6 (pbk.)
    1. Thoreau, Henry David, 1817-1862. Walden. 2. Environmental literature--History and criticism. 3. Environmental protection in literature. I. Wiener, Gary.
    PS3048.E58 2010
    818'.303--dc22

                                                                2009040566

Printed in the United States of America
2 3 4 5 6 7 14 13 12 11 10

Contents

Chapter 1: Background on Henry David Thoreau

Chapter 2: *Walden* and the Environment

Introduction

In the early twenty-first century, appeals for green living confront people daily—whether on television, through the Internet, or in newspapers and magazines. With warnings both nebulous and dire about global warming, man-made pollution, and animal extinction cropping up almost daily, the environment has become a fixed part of national discussions and debate, and most people are eager to learn about the small changes they can make to lower their carbon footprint.

Such beliefs, however, were entirely foreign in the 1840s when Henry David Thoreau set up camp at Walden Pond for two years, two months, and two days, initiating his quest for independent living on the symbolic date of July 4. To many of his neighbors, the eccentric Thoreau would most certainly have been characterized as an environmental wacko, if such a term had existed in 1845. Instead, he was labeled "that terrible Thoreau" and "The Hermit of Walden Woods." In fact, the genesis of *Walden; or, Life in the Woods* (1854), stems from his neighbors' curiosity about his aberrant lifestyle.

Giving a lecture in his hometown of Concord, Massachusetts, Thoreau was informed that his listeners were much more interested in exactly what he was doing out there in the middle of the woods all by himself. In twenty-first-century jargon, Thoreau might simply have told these busybodies that he was lowering his carbon footprint. In nineteenth-century terms, he gave the world *Walden*, his brilliant treatise on how to escape what he saw as the quiet desperation that was the lot of most human beings by drawing closer to nature and living the simple life. As novelist and fellow New Englander John Updike has written, only partly tongue in cheek, "*Walden* has become such a totem of the back-to-nature, preservationist, anti-business, civil-disobedience mindset, and Thoreau so vivid a protester, so perfect a crank and hermit saint, that the book risks being as revered and unread as the *Bible.*"

However eccentric, Thoreau was not quite the loner and hermit that some depictions have made him out to be. At Walden Pond, he was only a of couple miles from the heart of town, and he made numerous social trips to Concord in addition to welcoming visitors to his cabin near the pond. But his unique brand of environmental activism certainly brought him near the lunatic fringe in the eyes of his neighbors. Even his mentor, Ralph Waldo Emerson, not fully understanding his pupil, lamented that Thoreau had wasted his talents and his time. In Emerson's famous appraisal, he could not "help counting it a fault in him [Thoreau] that he had no ambition. Wanting this, instead of engineering for all America, he was the captain of a huckleberry party."

Emerson, of course, did not live long enough to realize the enormous sway Thoreau would someday command. His environmental philosophy and his politics influenced some of the world's greatest humanitarians, as evidenced by the impact his famous 1849 essay on nonviolence, "Resistance to Civil Government" (popularly known as "Civil Disobedience"), had on such leaders as Mahatma Gandhi and Martin Luther King Jr. Perhaps, then, Thoreau "engineered" not only for America but for all the world. Nowadays it is commonplace to characterize any unique historical figure as being ahead of his time. Thoreau truly was. Ironically, it was Emerson himself who said, "To be great is to be misunderstood."

A brief anecdote serves to sum up Thoreau's attitude toward nature as well as toward his neighbors in Concord. Returning from the woods one Sunday morning, carrying a pine tree that he intended to transplant, Thoreau passed by the meetinghouse just as worshippers were emerging. When his aunt Louisa scolded him for flouting convention so boldly, Thoreau simply replied, "I have been worshipping in my way and I don't trouble you in your way."

For Thoreau, the beauty and genuineness of the natural environment were worthy of his prayer, and one could pattern one's life on such principles. "Every morning," he wrote in *Walden*, "was a cheerful invitation to make my life of equal simplicity, and I may say innocence, with Nature herself." Many, from environmentalists to adventurers to self-styled societal rebels, have attempted to follow in Thoreau's footsteps. As Updike rightly notes, "Thoreau would not scorn contemporary efforts to effect his gospel and follow his example. *Walden* aims at conversion." According to Thoreau, modern life, whether in the nineteenth or twenty-first century, robs people of their best selves, and strong medicine is needed to restore that sense of individualism:

> We need the tonic of wildness,—to wade sometimes in marshes where the bittern and the meadow-hen lurk, and hear the booming of the snipe; to smell the whispering sedge where only some wilder and more solitary fowl builds her nest, and the mink crawls with its belly close to the ground. At the same time that we are earnest to explore and learn all things, we require that all things be mysterious and unexplorable, that land and sea be infinitely wild, unsurveyed and unfathomed by us because unfathomable. We can never have enough of Nature.

Like his mentor, Ralph Waldo Emerson, Thoreau here clearly acknowledges that humans and nature must coexist and that living in harmony with nature has untold benefits. As Professor Wesley T. Mott (organizer of the Ralph Waldo Emerson Society in 1989) has written, "Thoreau desired neither a hermit's isolation in the wilderness nor sentimental nature-worship. The issue was balance. When we save nature, he thought, we save ourselves. 'Nature,' he reminds us, 'is but another name of health.'"

Yet in the preceding Thoreau is breaking from Emerson and anticipating twenty-first-century ecologists and radical environmentalists. Emerson had an anthropocentric view of the natural world: nature was important inasmuch as it served the human need to grow and blossom. For Thoreau, "in wildness is the preservation of the world." Though the exact meaning of this phrase is still hotly debated today, many have argued that Thoreau is implying that nature is good in and of itself. As Professor Ann Woodlief of Virginia Commonwealth University writes, "Thoreau went on to explore the more recalcitrant facets of Nature's otherness, that wildness, as he called it, which had little or no correspondence with human needs or desires." It was enough that nature existed for its own sake, even at its most fearful and sublime. To the previous passage, Thoreau added,

> We must be refreshed by the sight of inexhaustible vigor, vast and Titanic features, the sea-coast with its wrecks, the wilderness with its living and its decaying trees, the thunder cloud, and the rain which lasts three weeks and produces freshets. We need to witness our own limits transgressed, and some life pasturing freely where we never wander.

It is not surprising then that today's environmentalists, both moderate and extreme, have embraced as a hero the man who, as posited by some, would let natural environments such as Walden Pond, ANWR in Alaska, or the South American rain forests exist solely for their own sake.

Thoreau was a man for all seasons; in *Walden* he takes readers through an entire year lived near to nature. As he gave his nineteenth-century contemporaries a model for living, so his *Walden* continues to provide readers with a blueprint for remaking their lives. Thoreau wants to live humbly, naturally, and, in his words, "deliberately, to front only the essential facts of life, and see if I could not learn what it had to teach, and not, when I came to die, discover that I had not lived."

The articles that follow show *Walden's* seminal place in the history of the environmental movement, suggesting why the book and its author have become so iconic in the debate over the natural world. These articles also suggest that the argument Thoreau launched in 1854 is more relevant than ever in this complex, modern world.

Chronology

July 12, 1817
David Henry Thoreau (later changed to Henry David Thoreau) is born in Concord, Massachusetts, to John and Cynthia (Dunbar) Thoreau.

1828
Thoreau enrolls at Concord Academy.

1833
Thoreau enters Harvard College.

1837
He graduates from Harvard.

1838
Thoreau starts a private school in Concord.

1839
Thoreau and his brother, John, travel the Concord and Merrimack rivers.

1840
Thoreau proposes to Ellen Sewall and is rejected. He publishes his first work in *The Dial*.

1841
Thoreau closes his school and moves into Ralph Waldo Emerson's home.

1842
Thoreau's brother, John, dies.

1843
Thoreau moves to New York City's Staten Island.

1844

He returns to Concord to work in the family pencil factory.

1845

Thoreau moves into his cabin on Walden Pond on July 4.

1846

Thoreau conceives of the idea for his book *Walden*. He takes his first trip to the Maine Woods. He spends a night in jail for refusing to pay poll tax.

1847

Thoreau leaves Walden Pond in the fall.

1848

Thoreau's essay on Maine, "Ktaadn," is published.

1849

A Week on the Concord and Merrimack Rivers and "Civil Disobedience" are published. Thoreau visits Cape Cod.

1850

Thoreau travels to Cape Cod again as well as to Canada.

1853

Thoreau makes a second trip to Maine.

1854

Walden; or, Life in the Woods is published.

1855

Thoreau makes a third trip to Cape Cod.

1856

Thoreau meets the poet Walt Whitman.

1857

Thoreau meets abolitionist John Brown. He makes his fourth trip to Cape Cod.

1859

Thoreau delivers "A Plea for Captain John Brown." After his father's death, he takes over the family pencil factory.

1861

Thoreau visits Minnesota as his illness worsens.

1862

Thoreau dies on May 6 and is buried in Sleepy Hollow Cemetery in Concord.

Social Issues in Literature

CHAPTER 1

Background on Henry David Thoreau

The Life of Henry David Thoreau

Walter Harding

Walter Harding taught at the State University of New York at Geneseo. An internationally recognized expert on Henry David Thoreau, Harding authored more than twenty books on the transcendentalist writer, including The Thoreau Handbook *and* The Days of Henry Thoreau: A Biography.

Harding states that for all of his worldliness, Henry David Thoreau rarely left Concord, Massachusetts, during his lifetime. A graduate of Harvard College, Thoreau early on found favor with the famous philosopher and writer Ralph Waldo Emerson, another Concord resident, and benefited greatly from Emerson's support. As Harding points out, though Thoreau was often dismissed as a second-rate imitator of Emerson and only published two books during his lifetime, A Week on the Concord and Merrimack Rivers *and* Walden, *he has since been universally acknowledged as one of America's greatest and most influential writers and thinkers.*

Generally unrecognized in his own day or, worse, dismissed as a second-rate imitator of his friend and mentor Ralph Waldo Emerson, Henry David Thoreau, in the twentieth century, has emerged as one of America's greatest literary figures. *Walden*, his account of two years spent living in a cabin on the shore of a pond in his native Concord, is universally recognized as the preeminent piece of American nature writing, though it is far more than simply a nature book. "Civil Disobedience," the account of and justification for his night spent

Walter Harding, *Dictionary of Literary Biography Vol. 1: The American Renaissance in New England, First Series*. Belmont, CA: Gale, 1978. Introduction and annotations copyright © 1997 by Bill McKibben. All rights reserved. Reproduced by permission of Gale, a part of Cengage Learning.

in jail in Concord in protest against slavery, particularly through its influence on such activists as Mahatma Gandhi and Martin Luther King [Jr.], has had wider political impact around the world than any other American literary document. As a prose stylist, Thoreau has been acknowledged by writers as disparate as Robert Louis Stevenson, Marcel Proust, Sinclair Lewis, and Henry Miller to be their master. As the apostle of the simple life, and the advocate of "listening to a different drummer," Thoreau is the hero of many of today's younger generation.

Youth and Education

Henry David Thoreau was born on 12 July 1817 in Concord, Massachusetts, eighteen miles northwest of Boston, the only member of the so-called "Concord School of Writers" to be a native of that town. Although both his paternal and maternal ancestors had once been prosperous, the family patrimony had dwindled away and, thanks to his father John Thoreau's financial ineptness, Thoreau himself was brought up in an atmosphere of genteel poverty. The family, with its four children—Helen (born 1812), John (born 1815), Henry, and Sophia (born 1819)—moved frequently from house to house (for a time living in nearby Chelmsford and in Boston), and the father from job to job, until in 1823 they returned to Concord and established a moderately successful pencil-making business. The children were educated in the Concord public schools and later, at their mother's insistence and at some financial sacrifice, in the more adequate and prestigious private Concord Academy. Henry, a shy and quiet youth, spent much time by himself wandering in the woods and fields of Concord, a proclivity encouraged by his mother, who often took the family on long walks to observe the wonders of nature.

By 1833 the family was somewhat more prosperous and with the financial help of his older brother and sister and of his maiden aunts, Thoreau entered Harvard College. Spending a good deal of his time reading in the college library, the first good collection of books he had had access to, he did become gregarious enough to join a fraternity (apparently chiefly to have access to *its* library) and take part in debates and colloquiums. In the winter of 1835–1836, to solve his financial problems, he dropped out for a time and taught school in Canton, Massachusetts, and again in the spring of 1836, he dropped out because of what was apparently an early attack of the tuberculosis that was to plague his life. Despite these absences, he maintained a better than average scholastic record and at his graduation in 1837 was chosen as one of the honor students to speak on the "Commercial Spirit," at the commencement exercises wherein he startled his audience by suggesting, "The order of things should be somewhat reversed; the seventh should be man's day of toil, wherein to earn his living by the sweat of his brow; and the other six his Sabbath of the affections and the soul,—in which to range this widespread garden, and drink in the soft influences and sublime revelations of nature"—a program of life which he himself was soon to adopt.

Thoreau as Teacher

Although the country was in the midst of a deep depression with a high unemployment rate, Thoreau was fortunate in being hired immediately by the Concord school committee to teach in the same one-room school he had attended as a child. However, within two weeks he had resigned rather than fulfill the committee's insistence on using corporal punishment and for nearly a year searched fruitlessly for another teaching position. Finally in the early summer of 1838 he established a private school in his home, with out-of-town pupils boarding with his mother. The school quickly prospered even though he used educational techniques that anticipated the "progressive education" of a century later. His brother soon joined him

Dismissed during his lifetime as an imitation of his mentor, Ralph Waldo Emerson, Thoreau is now considered among America's greatest and most influential writers. © Bettmann/ Corbis.

in the teaching and they rented the Concord Academy building to accommodate larger classes. The school eventually came to an end in 1841, when John's poor health forced him to drop out and Henry did not wish to continue the teaching alone.

Emerson's Influence and Aid

While Thoreau had been away to college, Ralph Waldo Emerson moved to Concord to live. Just when they first became acquainted is problematical, but by October of 1837 Emerson had asked Thoreau if he kept a daily journal, a practice which Emerson himself had long followed, and Thoreau embarked on that project which was to last to within a few months of his death a quarter of a century later and which was to fill nearly forty manuscript volumes with one of the most complete records of man's life and thought that we have. Begun primarily, as was Emerson's, as a source book for literary works, it eventually became, as we will see, a work of art in itself.

Emerson, thirteen years older and already nationally famous, took an immediate interest in his young friend, encouraging him to develop his literary talents, introducing him to his fellow Transcendentalists and to men and women of prominence in literary and publishing circles. After the closing of the Thoreau school, Emerson invited Thoreau to live in his home, helping thus to free him for further literary endeavors, and with the establishment of the *Dial* in 1840, providing him with an outlet for publication. Later this friendship was to wear thin, particularly when critics began charging Thoreau with being an imitator of Emerson (a charge which Emerson vigorously denied but which nonetheless embarrassed and annoyed Thoreau), and when Emerson's radicalism waned as Thoreau's waxed. But the rupture was never complete, and it was Emerson who gave the eulogy at Thoreau's funeral.

In the summer of 1839 Thoreau met Ellen Sewall of Scituate, Massachusetts, the sister of one of his school pupils and granddaughter of his mother's star boarder, Mrs. Joseph Ward. Henry fell in love with her, only to discover his brother John was in love with her too. John eventually proposed marriage and was rejected. Henry then too proposed and although Ellen was obviously attracted to him, she deferred to her father's wishes (he, a conservative Unitarian minister, was horrified at the thought of an associate of the "radical" Emerson for a son-in-law) and rejected him too. Although on his deathbed, Thoreau professed that he had always loved her, the whole "romance" has, as [Yale professor] Henry Seidel Canby once suggested, the air of "an experiment in the philosophy of love" on Thoreau's part about it. It was the only "romance" of his life.

In the spring of 1843, anxious to further Thoreau's position in the literary world, Emerson made arrangements for Henry to become the tutor of his brother William's sons on Staten Island. Thoreau did get to know a number of the New York City literati, most notably Horace Greeley, the editor of the *New-York Tribune*, then the nation's leading newspaper. Greeley was sufficiently impressed that he volunteered to be Thoreau's literary agent and not only over the years placed a number of his essays in leading journals of the time, but touted him frequently in the pages of the *Tribune*. But Thoreau was not happy on Staten Island. William Emerson had little of his brother's warmth or idealism and Thoreau was chronically homesick for Concord. After only six months he returned home and never left Concord again for any extended period of time. . . .

Moving to Walden Pond

Brother John Thoreau's tragic death by lockjaw in 1842 had a traumatic effect on Henry. For some weeks thereafter he himself experienced all the symptoms of lockjaw sympathetically, but eventually recovered, though he was never to hear John's name mentioned thereafter without tears coming to his eyes. In the later summer of 1839, he and John had taken a vacation rowboat trip on the Concord and Merrimack Rivers and now he determined to write an elegiac account of that trip as a tribute to his brother. To give himself the necessary time, in the spring of 1845 he persuaded Emerson to let him build a cabin on some newly acquired land on the shores of Walden Pond, a small glacial pond two miles south of Concord village, and there for two years, two months, and two days, he devoted himself to writing that book, observing the circling of the seasons, and living the simple life. His cabin (contrary to popular opinion, a sturdy, well-built structure, plastered and shingled) cost him $28.12 [frac12] and his living expenses 27¢ a week. Six weeks of work a year covered all his needs; the rest of his time was his own to live, to write, and to observe. The resulting book, *A Week on the Concord and Merrimack Rivers*, however, found little favor with publishers and did not reach print until in 1849 he guaranteed James Munroe and Company of Boston to reimburse any loss. One thousand copies were printed but when in 1853 Munroe found only 200 copies had been sold (and seventy-five given away), they shipped the remainder to Thoreau to clear their shelves. (Thoreau that night wrote in his Journal, "I have now a library of nearly nine hundred volumes, over seven hundred of which I wrote myself."). . .

Thoreau's Night in Jail

Concord, appropriately enough since it was the site of the first battle of the American Revolution, was a hotbed of anti-slavery agitation. Thoreau's mother and sisters were active members of the Concord Female Anti-Slavery Society and their house was an active station on the Underground Railroad aiding slaves in their flight to freedom in Canada. Thoreau himself both approved and assisted in these activities. In 1843 his friend and fellow-Concordian Amos Bronson Alcott (father of the Louisa May Alcott of *Little Women* fame), who too was an ardent Abolitionist, refused to pay his poll tax in Concord as a protest against the legality of slavery in the South. Alcott was arrested but freed before he could be jailed because a neighbor insisted on paying the tax over his protest. The incident provoked Thoreau's thought: Was serving in the

Underground Railroad doing enough? Why not directly confront the government that legalized slavery? So he too refused to pay his poll tax. The local tax collector, constable, and jailer Samuel Staples delayed taking action until one evening late in July of 1846, meeting Thoreau on the main street of Concord (Thoreau had come in from Walden Pond to take a shoe to the cobbler), Staples inquired when Thoreau would pay the tax and even offered to pay it for him if Thoreau was short of funds. Thoreau replied that he was not paying it as a matter of principle. When Staples in turn replied that he would eventually have to arrest him, Thoreau said, "You might as well do it right now," and Staples led him off to jail. Late that evening someone (it is generally thought to have been Thoreau's maiden aunt Maria Thoreau who, though an Abolitionist herself, was shocked to find a nephew in jail) paid his tax for him, and the next morning Staples went to the jail to release him. To Staples's amazement, Thoreau objected strenuously, and left the jail only when Staples threatened to throw him out bodily; it had been his intent to challenge the legality of slaves in the courts and his release from jail effectively deprived him of that opportunity. (It is generally believed that Aunt Maria paid his tax in advance in following years depriving him of any *later* opportunity.) When curious neighbors pestered him with questions as to why he *wanted* go to jail, Thoreau finally wrote out an explanation of his position and delivered it to his fellow townsmen as a two-part lecture at the local Concord Lyceum on 26 January and 16 February 1848 on "The Rights and the Duties of the Individual in Relation to Government." A year later, when Elizabeth Peabody was preparing her first (and only) issue of *Aesthetic Papers*, a periodical she hoped would carry on the tradition of the deceased *Dial*, she persuaded Thoreau to let her print the lecture there and it appeared under the title "Resistance to Civil Government." (It was not until 1866, four years after Thoreau's death, when it was gathered into one of his posthumous collections of essays, *A Yankee in Canada, with Anti-Slavery and Reform Papers*, that it was given the title "Civil Disobedience" by which it is best known.). . . .

Thoreau had long been active in the Concord Lyceum, which sponsored a series of lectures in Concord each winter. He attended it as a boy and after returning to Concord from college both occasionally served as its "curator" or secretary and read his own lectures from its platform. As we have seen with "Civil Disobedience," it often served as a trying out place for his essays. . . .

Walden

When on 4 February 1846, while living at Walden Pond, he delivered a lecture on Thomas Carlyle at the Concord Lyceum, some in his audience told him that they would rather hear about his life at the pond than about an obscure Englishman. A year later, heeding that advice, he delivered a lecture on "The History of Myself," and it was so well received that he followed it with further accounts of his life at Walden, a series of lectures that eventually grew into his masterwork, *Walden*. A first version of the book was completed by the time he left the pond in the fall of 1847, and when he published *A Week* [*A Week on the Concord and Merrimack Rivers*] in 1849, he announced therein the forth-coming publication of *Walden*. But *A Week*'s failure was so complete that no publisher would risk issuing a second book by Thoreau. Thoreau, however, was not daunted; he simply went to work revising and revising again his new book. By 1854 when it was finally published, it had gone through seven complete revisions and was a very different book. Had not *A Week* been such a failure, it is conceivable that Thoreau would never have done the revising and rewriting that eventually made *Walden* the great book it is. . . .

Walden was published in 1854 by Ticknor & Fields in Boston in an edition of 2,000 copies. It was more widely and generally more favorably reviewed than *A Week*, though at least one reviewer denounced him [Thoreau] as "a rural humbug." It took five years however to sell out that first edition and it was not reprinted until after his death in 1862.

While living at Walden Pond in 1846, Thoreau took an "excursion," as he liked to call it, to the wilds of the Maine Woods with his cousin George Thatcher, canoeing its rivers and, by himself, climbing Katahdin, Maine's highest mountain—in fact, being one of the first ever to reach its summit. . . .

Leaving Walden Pond

When in the late summer of 1847 Emerson accepted an invitation to give a lengthy series of lectures in England, he was in a quandary about leaving his ailing wife and three small children at home alone. Lidian Emerson suggested that would Thoreau but leave Walden and come back to live with them, their problem would be solved. Thoreau, who was beginning to fear he was in a rut at the pond, particularly since he had completed first drafts of both *A Week* and *Walden*, accepted their invitation and abandoned his cabin. He remained in the Emerson household for a year and then, on Emerson's return from England, went back to living with his parents, where he remained for the rest of his life. He did not, however, in principle abandon the life he had led at Walden. He continued to devote his mornings to writing, his afternoons to nature, and he still lived a simple enough life that six weeks of work a year covered all his expenses. Surveying became probably his major source of income, but he still worked occasionally in his father's pencil factory, and was not above doing almost any sort of menial labor if and when he needed the cash. . . .

Anti-Slavery Activities

With the passage of the Fugitive Slave Law in 1850 and the approach of the Civil War, the controversy over slavery became more and more embittered. When in 1854, a fugitive slave, Anthony Burns, was captured in Boston and forced to return to slavery in the South, Thoreau felt impelled to strike out. He attended an anti-slavery gathering in nearby Framingham and there delivered his "Slavery in Massachusetts," a scathing attack not only on the slave-owners in the South but on those in the North who, through their inertia and willingness to go along, enabled slavery to continue in the South. "My thoughts are murder to the State," he cried out in this, perhaps his most polemical, essay. Five years later, when John Brown led his attack on Harper's Ferry, hoping thereby to instigate a mass revolt of the slaves, many of Thoreau's friends were appalled at the audacity of his act, but not Thoreau. He saw Brown as a man who was willing to sacrifice his own life for a principle. Against the advice of even the Abolitionists, Thoreau called a public meeting in Concord Town Hall, rang the bell himself when the selectmen of the town refused to announce the meeting, and in an impassioned voice read his "Plea for Captain John Brown," winning over to his viewpoint a primarily hostile audience. Later he repeated the lecture at Boston and Worcester. On the day of Brown's hanging, he, with friends, conducted a memorial service in Concord where he read "The Last Days of John Brown," and when Brown was buried in North Elba, New York, the next summer, sent another memorial paper, "After the Death of John Brown," to be read there. But the John Brown incident paradoxically marked the end of Thoreau's anti-slavery activities. A little more than a year later, Thoreau was a seriously ill man. . . .

Illness and Death

In early December of 1860, Thoreau caught a bad cold and when, against doctor's orders, he refused to cancel a lecture engagement in Waterbury, Connecticut, it worsened into bronchitis. He had been plagued from college days with recurring flare-ups of tuberculosis (or "consumption" as it was then called). The bronchitis brought on a recurrence of the tuberculosis and doctors told him his only hope for recovery was to remove to a drier climate. In May of 1861 he set out for Minnesota with Horace Mann, Jr., son of the famed educator, but it was soon obvious that he had waited too long and after two months of desultory wandering in the upper Middle West, including a visit to a Sioux tribal gathering on the upper reaches of the Minnesota River, he returned to Concord reconciled to an early death. He spent the last months of his life revising old papers (thus many of Thoreau's essays exist in two versions, an original and a revised text) and piecing together unfinished works. The major accomplishment of this period perhaps was the conversion to essay form of a lecture he had been delivering for a number of years under various titles and which is now known as "Life Without Principle." It is the capstone of his writing career and in highly concentrated form presents the most significant aspects of his philosophy of life. Too intense, perhaps, to make a good introduction to Thoreau, it does make a superb summing up and is one of the favorite essays of most ardent Thoreauvians.

Thoreau faced death with a remarkable cheerfulness (said by some medical authorities to be characteristic of those dying of tuberculosis). When a more orthodox aunt asked if he had made his peace with God, he replied that he had never quarreled with Him. When a deacon asked him about "that other world," he replied, "One world at a time." When he became too weak to write, he dictated to his sister Sophia. In his last few days he made an heroic effort to complete his Maine Woods papers. When he died on the morning of 6 May 1862 his last words were "moose" and "Indian." He is buried in Sleepy Hollow Cemetery in Concord, on "Authors' Ridge" close to the graves of his friends Emerson, Alcott, Hawthorne, and Ellery Channing.

Thoreau Spoke of the Environment in a Way That Made People Listen

Laura Dassow Walls

Laura Dassow Walls has taught at Lafayette College and is professor and Chair of Southern Letters at the University of South Carolina. Her books include Emerson's Life in Science: The Culture of Truth *and, with coeditor Sandra Harbert Petrulionis,* More Day to Dawn: Thoreau's "Walden" for the Twenty-first Century.

Henry David Thoreau is among the most eloquent and convincing American nature writers, writes Walls. His words helped to launch the American environmental movement that has continued to this day. Walls explains that Thoreau both celebrated and feared the "wild" in nature, and long before it became a popular notion, he understood that nature was an independent entity from humankind that could exist and thrive without human intervention. As a romantic thinker, Thoreau believed that each individual must forge a life in harmony with nature—his or her own individual "Walden"—that would lead to self-growth and personal fulfillment.

The West of which I speak is but another name for the Wild; and what I have been preparing to say is, that in Wildness is the preservation of the World.

No doubt there would have been an environmental movement without Thoreau, but it is hard to imagine such a movement without the rhetorical fire of his words or the inspirational force of his actions. It was Thoreau's ability to embody his actions in powerful and incisive language that made them resonate so widely: most famously, his one-night stand in a Concord jail, the consequence of his non-payment of the tax which supported war in Mexico and slavery in the South; and his residence for two years, two months and two days at Walden Pond, a deep glacier-cut lake just a mile from town. The writings that resulted crystallized concepts that helped shape the actions of generations of successors: anger over his night in jail kindled Thoreau's protest essay 'Resistance to Civil Government', which gave Mohandas Gandhi the term 'civil disobedience'; and joy in his sojourn at Walden Pond suffused *Walden* with poetic energy, making this the defining event of Thoreau's life and career as a writer. In *Walden*, Thoreau moves from caustic criticism of American society to a lyrical intimacy with nature, teaching him, and us, how the spirit of the one can redeem us from the evils of the other. Thoreau's writings became the touchstone for a new and deeper valuation of nature which led, in the decades after his death, to the beginnings of the environmental movement in the USA, starting with Ralph Waldo Emerson and John Muir. As Lawrence Buell writes, thousands of devotees have made pilgrimages to Walden Pond and Thoreau has become our 'environmental hero', the father of American nature writing.

Thoreau at Walden

Thoreau was hardly born a naturalist. As a child he joined in family outings into the countryside around Concord, Massachusetts, a small farming village and county seat, set in a rolling landscape of farms, lakes, rivers and second-growth woodlands. Apart from these rambles, Thoreau showed no special disposition towards nature study. His education at Harvard [College] turned him into an accomplished scholar of Greek and Latin, well prepared for his intended profession of schoolteaching. When their notions proved too progressive for the established schools, Henry and his elder brother John opened a school of their own, which flourished briefly until John's ill health forced them to close it in 1841. Henry's life took a further turn when John died suddenly of lockjaw, in January 1842. In the years that followed, Henry tried various ways of making a living: as a tutor, a handyman, assistant in his father's pencil factory and surveyor; but with the encouragement of his friend Ralph Waldo Emerson and the 'Transcendental' movement he inspired, Thoreau set his sights on literature as his true vocation. In 1844, Emerson bought land on Walden Pond, and in 1845, with Emerson's blessing, Thoreau began to build his cabin. When he moved in—on Independence Day, 4 July 1845—Thoreau took with him the materials for his first major writing project, *A Week on the Concord and Merrimack Rivers* (1849), a meditative re-telling of a two-week journey he and John had taken in 1839. While at the Pond, though, Thoreau began gathering materials for his next project, *Walden*. At first he merely sought to explain his unusual actions to his curious fellow-townsmen, but over the years the project grew to encompass the events of his stay at the pond and the philosophy of living he learned to practise on its shores.

It was while he was living at the Pond that Thoreau was seized and jailed, one afternoon in July 1846 when he was running errands in town. The controversy that ensued sharpened his political thought; already a vocal abolitionist and a modest success on the lecture circuit, from the 1840s onwards Thoreau was increasingly prominent as an anti-slavery speaker and activist. Two other events at the Pond also shaped his future career. First, a few weeks after his arrest Thoreau travelled to Maine, where on Mount Katahdin he first encountered true wilderness. The experience, as he narrated it in 'Ktaadn', shattered his image of nature as a safe and nurturing mother: here, 'Vast, Titanic, inhuman Nature' seemed to corner him and query, 'why came ye here before your time? This ground is not prepared for you.' It was difficult, Thoreau pondered, 'to

Ralph Waldo Emerson, Thoreau's mentor, gives a lecture to a large audience during a meeting of the Summer School of Philosophy. The school was established by Emerson, Thoreau, Bronson Alcott, and other Transcendentalists. © Bettmann/Corbis.

conceive of a region uninhabited by man', for we presume our presence 'everywhere. And yet we have not seen pure Nature, unless we have seen her thus vast, and drear, and inhuman . . . Here was no man's garden, but the unhandselled globe.' After this revelation, Thoreau could see that even Walden's peaceful landscape held its terrors, for some element in nature was always and irreducibly Other: or, as he would soon call it, Wild.

Thoreau's Influences

The second event suggested one way in which that otherness might be approached, if not fully comprehended. As Thoreau increasingly turned to nature, he also turned to writings about nature, especially to works of natural history. But the arrival in Boston of Louis Agassiz, the famous Swiss natural scientist, turned Thoreau from observer to participant. Agassiz soon organized a collecting network, and by April 1847 Thoreau was shipping specimens of fish, turtles, and even a fox, to Agassiz, who declared some of the species Thoreau collected new to science. Soon afterwards, Thoreau came to the writings of Agassiz's mentor, [German naturalist] Alexander von Humboldt, and of [British naturalist] Charles Darwin and [Scottish geologist] Charles Lyell, also deeply influenced by Humboldt. Thoreau was critical of natural history surveys, which he condemned as 'inventories of God's property, by some clerk'—but here was something else again, a cosmic vision of nature as one great whole to be approached through the loving and exacting study of its myriads of details, not in the laboratory but out in the wild, through exploration and collection. Thoreau caught the Humboldtian wave just as it was cresting, not only in Europe but in America, where Humboldtian science was stimulating the organization and funding of government-sponsored Exploring Expeditions to the American West and along the coastlines of North and South America. Humboldt promoted a science that included organism and environment in one interconnected web, a synthesis that decades later would be named 'ecology'. Thoreau's discovery of proto-ecological science was of tremendous importance to his development as a thinker, for in it he found tools and models for conducting his own 'ecological' studies of the Concord environment. By the early 1850s, this new vocation absorbed most of his productive hours, including the records in his *Journal*, which eventually totalled over two million words. Under the excitement of his emerging passion, *Walden*—which had languished in manuscript form since the commercial failure of *A Week*—grew to maturity.

Thoreau's Nature Books

Published at last in 1854, *Walden* remains the classic text at the head of all American nature writing since. It is directed to all those who recognize that, like the 'mass of men', they too 'lead lives of quiet desperation'. Thoreau's 'experiment' at Walden Pond sheds all but the essential trappings of 'civilized' life to reveal a more truly civil life of the mind, lived close to nature's rhythms and attentive to her creatures, of whom we are, of course, one. 'Not till we are lost, in other words, not till we have lost the world, do we begin to find ourselves, and realize where we are and the infinite extent of our relations', Thoreau wrote. Walden is above all a place to dwell and 'find' oneself, and so the emphasis in *Walden* is on domestic nature. Two other works, which overlap in the time of their composition but which were not published in final form until after Thoreau's death, take up the nature of wilderness and of those whose lives border civilized and wild. *The Maine Woods* (1864) collects the narratives of Thoreau's three trips to Maine: 'Ktaadn' was followed by 'Chesuncook', in which Thoreau joins a moose hunt, and 'The Allegash and East Branch', in which he considers the mind and life of the Indian through his friendship with the Penobscot guide Joe Polis. In *Cape Cod* (1865), Thoreau visits the men and women who live in the dunes with the sea at their backs, and here, facing that sea, Thoreau considers that 'wilderness reaching round the globe, wilder than a Bengal jungle, and fuller of monsters'. Thoreau's beach delineates, like Mount Katahdin, the outermost edge of humanity and holds similar terrors: 'It is a wild rank place, and there is no flattery in it . . . There is naked Nature— inhumanly sincere, wasting no thought on man, nibbling at the cliffy shore where gulls wheel amid the spray.'

An Environmentalist's Life Cut Short

Thoreau's early death, at age 44, cut short the developing projects of what should have been his middle years. Thoreau was well on his way to a unique synthesis of scientific precision with a poet's love of metaphor. Most notably, 'The Succession of Forest Trees' (1860) presents both a scientific theory accounting for patterns of forest succession and a passionate argument for intelligent forest management. The need for such an argument reminds us that Thoreau's home landscape was hardly pristine: already in the 1840s it had been worn down by 200 years of European use. Furthermore, the onset of the Industrial Revolution alerted Thoreau to its long-term consequences: the railroad had cut across a corner of Walden just before he moved there, and cutting timber for ties and fuel had by the 1850s nearly levelled the forests he grew up with. Once-familiar species like deer and beaver had long been hunted out of his neighbourhood, and his critique of capitalism included the fear that soon all open land would be fenced and posted against trespassers, outlawing the kind of long cross-country walks he took daily. In another of his late essays, 'Wild Apples', Thoreau warned against the coming of the evil days when 'even all the trees of the field, are withered'. Yet he did not counsel despair. Instead, Thoreau began to work out solutions whereby the community would combine to create 'national preserves', taking selected lands out of the system of private property and holding them in trust for all, 'a common possession forever, for instruction and recreation'. Such land, if forested, was not to be cut but to 'stand and decay for higher uses', suggesting an ethic of preservation; in another late manuscript, Thoreau speculated that 'Forest wardens should be appointed by the town' to oversee the management of private woodlots. Americans had much to learn, Thoreau suggested, from the English, who 'have taken great pains to learn how to create forests', where Americans still bushwhack infant forests or foolishly plough them underground. Thus the seeds of the two contending sides of the environmental movement—preservation of resources and their conservation or managed use—may both be found in Thoreau's late writings.

A Belief in the Primacy of Nature

Though he was active in educating his townspeople about better ways to live with the land and the river, Thoreau never sponsored or joined what could be called a 'movement', in environmental activism or anything else. His reasoning is presented in 'Resistance to Civil Government', where political change is shown to emerge from the convergent actions of all persons with a conscience who, based on their independent moral reasoning, refuse to participate in social injustice. As Emerson had written in 'Self-Reliance', the true reformer 'is weaker by every recruit to his banner'. Thoreau pushed Emerson's idea of self-reliant resistance even farther: first, for Thoreau, nature, too, has the power to 'resist' humankind. That is, nature is not plastic in our hands, to mould as we wish; physical nature has the power to push back, against our designs, or is simply indifferent to them, like the Titan of 'Ktaadn' or the world-circling ocean. When Thoreau looked at wild creatures, they looked back at him, and what he saw in their eyes was not his own reflection but something alien, 'wild'. Thus for Thoreau nature had its own moral standing: 'Who hears the fishes when they cry?', he asked of the shad trapped before the Billerica dam; and he went on to warn, 'It will not be forgotten by some memory that we were contemporaries'. Thoreau understood that were humans removed, nature would still exist and she would not mourn. That insight, astonishing for its time, both fascinated and frightened Thoreau, who was fundamentally a humanist in his outlook; that the universe might be *bio*centric was both troubling and exciting to him. As a result, he attended to the relationship between humans and their environment in a way that few were yet capable of imagining.

Changing One Mind at a Time

Second, Thoreau believed that power flowed from the individual to the collective. Emerson had entertained this idea, but like most Romantics he was even more taken by its complement, the way in which power flowed from the whole organization through the individual. Thoreau stubbornly lived his independent convictions in a way that unnerved his friends, but it was in this way that Thoreau joined his political ideals—his vision of the ultimate democracy—with his understanding of how nature worked: through a creative harmony of independent agents, each seeing to their own ends, but in their purposes borrowing each other to combine towards a higher whole. Thoreau's intellectual convictions also shaped his literary style: since the individual initiated social change, Thoreau sought to move each single reader. By turns he shocks, insults, mocks, jokes, disarms, reasons, preaches, contradicts and sings, knowing that while some readers will shake him off, others will be provoked and inspired. Above all, Thoreau knew the power of a good story, and so in *Walden* he tellingly offers a narrative of his own narrow escape from bondage to freedom. Of course, the point is lost if readers could not imagine recreating the story in their own lives, and so Thoreau invites his readers—us—to follow him, not to Walden Pond but to our own 'Walden', from which we might find our way to a life lived not in desperation but in wisdom.

For Thoreau, such a goal was inconceivable apart from nature: 'culture', the definitive characteristic of humanity, was a process of self-growth or 'cultivation' which joined human effort with the unworked natural landscape, changing both together—like Thoreau in his notorious Walden bean-field. We are not set into our environment; rather, we and our environment grow together into an interlinked whole, such that a careful look around will tell who, and what, we are. Thoreau's exacting observation of the landscape of Concord told him America still had a long way to go, that most human possibility still lay unrealized. If we are a little closer to the civil society he imagined, it is partly because he spoke, in a way that made us listen.

Thoreau Was a Poet-Naturalist

Stephen Hahn

Stephen Hahn has served as associate provost and professor of English at William Paterson University in Wayne, New Jersey. His books include Teaching Faulkner *and* On Derrida.

It is difficult to pin Henry David Thoreau down to one role in life, Hahn suggests, so to call him merely a naturalist understates his versatility. Thoreau himself did not like to be categorized and wrote that those who observe nature from one point of view, such as the botanist's, often miss the larger truths that are right before them. Thoreau approached natural science with a poet's mind-set, and, according to Hahn, in his numerous roles as walker, historian, excursionist, surveyor, gardener, and so on, Thoreau set a precedent for interdisciplinary inquiry long before this model became fashionable.

"We must look for a long time before we can see."— "Natural History of Massachusetts" (*Natural History Writings*)

The name "Thoreau" is nearly synonymous for many people with the word "nature," although they assume perhaps too easily that a book such as *Walden* is primarily about something we would commonly call nature—meaning water, trees, plants, soils, and undomesticated animals. . . . It is something more and other than that, even while those objects are part of what compose its referential world. Thoreau is a writer about nature, "improved" or cultivated and "unimproved" and wild, primarily in relation to the human presence in it. . . . In what sense and how he writes about nature in his "natural history" essays and his journals is as unique and individual as the manner in which he writes about other topics such as consciousness or social reform. At the same time, his style and approach in writing about nature is specifiable within a spectrum of approaches from the conventionally "poetic" to the "scientific," although nearly anyone's first impulse would be to identify him more strongly with the poetic. Indeed, there are times when Thoreau appears to disparage the scientific in favor of the poetic: "That is a scientific account of the fact," he writes of the chemical explanation or why leaves change color in the fall, "—only a reassertion of the fact"; and, "How differently the poet and the naturalist look at objects!"

Thoreau as a Man of Science

Not surprisingly for Thoreau, however, a stance that begins in disparagement and negation generally finds its way to the affirmation of a synthesis (albeit with the experiential and poetic dominating) between opposed terms. Thus, in his earliest published writing on natural history, he begins his closing paragraph in a mood of dejection: "These volumes deal much in measurements and minute descriptions, not interesting to the general reader, with only here and there a colored sentence to allure him, like those plants growing in dark forests, which bear only leaves without blossoms." He goes on, however, to encourage the reader: "Let us not underrate the value of a fact; it will one day flower into a truth." And then, noting how much of the natural history of "any animal" or "man himself" remains to be written, he as much as writes a job description for the "true" (and future) "man of science," balancing past and future as in the closing of so many works:

> Slow are the beginnings of philosophy. He has something
> demoniacal in him, who can discern a law or couple two
> facts. We can imagine a time when 'Water runs down hill'
> may have been taught in schools. The true man of science
> will know better by his finer organization; he will smell,

taste, see, hear, feel, better than other men. His will be a deeper and finer experience. We do not learn by inference and deduction, but by direct intercourse and sympathy. It is with science as with ethics,—we cannot know the truth by contrivance and method; the Baconian is as false as any other, and with all the helps of machinery and the arts, the most scientific will still be the healthiest and friendliest man, and possess a more perfect Indian wisdom. ("Natural History of Massachusetts")

Historians of science can refer us here, in tracing the idea of "coupl[ing] two facts" to the theory of "consilience" in which "Facts are not only brought together, but seen in a new point of view.... [And] a new mental Element is superinduced...," creating a "new conception," resulting from "a principle of connexion and unity, supplied by the mind." If Thoreau had not grasped this idea from [English scientist, philosopher, and theologian] William Whewell, then it was available to him even more directly in [English poet William] Wordsworth's famous formulation:

> Imagination ... has no reference to images that are merely a faithful copy, existing in the mind, of absent external objects; but is a word of higher import, denoting the operations of the mind upon those objects, and processes of creation or of fixed composition, governed by certain fixed laws.... Conferring additional properties upon an object, or abstracting from it some of those which it actually possesses ... thus enabling it to react upon the mind which hath performed the process, like a new existence. (Preface to *Poems*)

Poetry and Science

Regardless of where Thoreau got his phrasing and conception from, the effect of his peroration [conclusion to a speech] in "The Natural History of Massachusetts" is to steal back the idea of the "man of science" for the humanistic and integrative conception of science as opposed to a mechanistic and operationalist view. The parallel between Whewell and Wordsworth suggests a deeper parallel that it is possible to discern in modes of perception that lead to discovery through observation and reflection. (It is important to note that, in contrast to either Whewell or Wordsworth, Thoreau does not foreclose on the question of the origin of ideas, referring some to the external sensations or the memory of sensations and others to the mind alone. Even in referring to life as "a kind of fiction, a work of the imagination only" in *Walden*, he refers to the point of view of the aspect of the self he calls "the spectator." As we will see, Thoreau does not make the traditional, categorical division of man and nature.) The history of science no doubt bypassed this rhetorical moment of attempted reconciliation between poetry and science—among other reasons because of the burgeoning scientific activity spurred by the invention of devices for measurement and computation and the expanding fields they opened for inquiry. But, wisely, Thoreau had not denied the importance of "measurements and minute descriptions," only their lack of interest to the "general reader." Paradoxically, it was that lack of interest that most probably contributed to a lack of exploration of Thoreau's more strictly scientific writings after his death—some of which are only being winnowed out from his manuscripts several lifetimes later.

Finally, on the matter of the "man of science," it is not surprising to find that Thoreau also notes the effect of the division of labor and the professionalizing of what was to become not the "man of science" but the "scientist" (a word that did not gain general use until the mid-nineteenth century). Throughout his natural history writings, Thoreau comments on the harm that the division of labor does to our knowledge, so that knowledge of nature is a kind of triumph over abstraction and selection that results not from the play of the imagination but from a limitation of focus:

A man sees only what concerns him. A botanist absorbed in the study of grasses does not distinguish the grandest pasture oaks. He, as it were, tramples down oaks unwittingly in his walk, or at most only sees their shadows. (*Natural History Essays*)

He continues the illustration through several different sorts of persons and concerns, and he makes a similar point in the posthumously published essay "Huckleberries." Here he compares the view of the "professional huckleberry picker," landowner, cook, and ends with the botanist:

> While Professor D.—for whom the pudding is intended, sits in his library writing a book—a work on the *Vaccinieae* [huckleberry] of course. And now the result of this downward course will be seen in that work—which should be the ultimate fruit of the huckleberry field. It will be worthless. It will have none of the spirit of the huckleberry in it, and the reading of it will be a weariness of the flesh. I believe in a different kind of division of labor—that Professor D. should be encouraged to divide himself freely between his library and the huckleberry field.

Given Thoreau's desire that "there may be as many different persons in the world as possible," the point is not to disparage any particular persons but rather the sort of alienation that results when persons are, again, reduced to functions or to the status of things with a concomitant reduction of their field of perception. The desire for many different persons is in fact a desire for the expansion of perception, consistent with a view that unity exists in multiplicity and diversity, as in his parable of the mountain.

Thoreau's Shifting Roles

As we read Thoreau's natural history writings we find him shifting roles from poet to moralist to naturalist-observer to scientist with some fluidity, often within the same work. What remains consistent is the habit of observation which appears to become both more trained and more diversified over time. The sort of "seeing" that is implied in his assertion that "we must look a long time before we can see" is never identified with any particular vantage but with the training of perception to derive pleasure or knowledge, or pleasure and knowledge combined, from the objects of the beholder's attention. Because Thoreau often drew on prior writing—in his journals and in other works—it is, however, difficult to ascribe changes in approach to his "development" as a writer. It is less difficult to see them as allied to his varied roles in relation to nature: walker, historian, excursionist, surveyor, gardener, and leader of huckleberry parties. These roles allowed him to adopt purposeful or utilitarian approaches to nature, measuring and observing formal relationships in space and time as a surveyor; to ask questions about prior human presence in the landscape, as historian and excursionist; to note the periodicity of natural events by the calendar, as gardener and gatherer; to enjoy the esthetic effects of the natural scene, as walker; and to combine and shift among these modes or approaches almost at will. Overall, they led him to anticipate a sort of interdisciplinary model of inquiry even before the discrete modern disciplines were in fact laid out.

Thoreau Was an Ecologist Before There Was Ecology

Roderick Nash

Roderick Nash has served as professor of history and environmental studies at the University of California, Santa Barbara. He is a nationally recognized expert on resource management, wilderness preservation, and environmental education. Among his books are Wilderness and the American Mind *and, with Gregory Graves,* From These Beginnings: A Biographical Approach to American History.

In the nineteenth century, England was ahead of the United States in recognizing the rights of nature, observes Nash. Three reasons for this were the abundance of wilderness in the fledgling United States, the dominant concern of human rights and slavery, and the American notion that nature was here to serve humanity. Discussing nature's rights could only earn one the public's ridicule in Henry David Thoreau's time; according to Nash, this was one reason he was not recognized for his contributions to nature until well into the twentieth century. Thoreau, the transcendentalist, believed in the importance of everything on the planet, both human and nonhuman. In this sense, Nash explains, he took a "wider view of the universe" than did his contemporaries.

In the United States the greatest gains in conservation or environmentalism occurred after 1960. But in the eighteenth and nineteenth centuries England went far beyond her former colony in expounding an ethical philosophy of human-nature relationships and in beginning its legal implementation with respect to animals. There was no [English utilitarian philoso-

Roderick Frazier Nash, *The Rights of Nature: A History of Environmental Ethics*. Madison, WI: The University of Wisconsin Press, 1989. Copyright © 1989 by the Board of Regents of the University of Wisconsin System. Reproduced by permission.

pher] Jeremy Bentham or [animal rights activist] John Lawrence in the United States and no Martin's Act [to prevent cruelty to cattle]. The few Americans who did talk about nature in ethical terms in the nineteenth century were not even dignified by ridicule; most often, they were ignored completely. It is well to remember in this regard that Thoreau did not become an environmental hero until well into the twentieth century. Significantly, his modern reputation depended in large part on his discovery and popularization by English animal rightists, notably [Thoreau biographer] Henry S. Salt.

Reasons Why Nineteenth-Century Americans Ignored the Rights of Nature

With full awareness of the risks of broad cross-cultural generalizations, three observations help explain the lag time between American and English consideration of the rights of nature. First, for much of the nineteenth century the majority of territory claimed by the United States was wilderness. The inexhaustibility of resources was the dominant American myth for a century after independence. Even utilitarian conservation seemed unnecessary, much less any viewpoint that challenged anthropocentrism [that the human perspective is the only important perspective]. Even people critical of resource exploitation could not escape the feeling that there was, after all, plenty of room for people *and* nature in the New World. Consider, for instance, that until May 10, 1869, one could not cross the continent without having to go at least part of the way on foot or with the aid of animals. On May 24, 1869, two weeks after the first railroad linked the coasts, John Wesley Powell rode the new train to Green River, Wyoming, and started in boats down a thousand miles of unmapped river. The Indian wars were in full cry then; much of the West was wild. In this geographical context, progress seemed synonymous with growth, development, and the conquest of nature. The idea of living ethically and harmoniously with nature was incompatible with nineteenth-century American priorities.

A second reason for the lack of American interest in the rights of nature until well into the twentieth century was the dominant concern of earlier intellectuals and reformers with the rights of people. The Revolution released a flood of idealism based on natural-rights principles, but for a century it focused almost exclusively on social problems such as slavery. For almost a century after 1776, the oppression of black people diverted American eyes from other wrongs. As far as natural rights idealists were concerned, slavery was the firebell in the night that had to be answered first. It would have been incongruous for Congress to pass legislation forbidding cruelty to cattle while millions of human beings existed as unprotected livestock. So a Wendell Phillips or a William Lloyd Garrison [both American abolitionists] devoted himself to abolitionism. In England, on the other hand, slavery was on the way to legal abolition in 1792, and a John Lawrence or a Richard Martin could turn his attention to righting other kinds of wrong.

Third, when Americans at last began protecting nature in the nineteenth century, it was through a very anthropocentrically defined national park ideal. Americans preserved Yellowstone (1872), the Adirondacks (1885), and Yosemite (1890) for people's pleasure and for utilitarian purposes such as water and game supply. England in the same period had no wilderness and consequently directed its environmental ideals to a component of nature closer to its experience: animals, especially domesticated ones. Henry Salt's Humanitarian League and [American naturalist] John Muir's Sierra Club, founded within a year of each other in the early 1890s, had vastly different objectives related to the particular experience of their respective cultures with nature.

An Ecologist Before Ecology

In choosing the Fourth of July for his 1845 departure to Walden Pond, Henry David Thoreau intended to make what a later generation would call a "statement." The Massachusetts naturalist-philosopher saw little to celebrate about his nation's first sixty-nine years. Americans seemed to be obsessed with what his Concord colleague, Ralph Waldo Emerson, called "things." Going to a shop to buy a blank notebook in which to record his thoughts, Thoreau could only find ledgers ruled for dollars and cents. His countrymen appeared to be oblivious to any but utilitarian values. Nature was merely an object—a resource—and they exploited it with a vengeance. Thoreau observed the rapid recession of the New England forest and commented: "Thank God, men cannot as yet fly, and lay waste the sky as well as the earth!" He was one of the first Americans to perceive inexhaustibility as a myth.

As [writer] Donald Worster has explained, there were ecologists before "ecology." Thoreau was among them. The word itself dates to 1866, but the idea that the many parts of nature fit together into a single unit—or were so fitted by a creative God—[has] appeared frequently in scientific and religious circles since the seventeenth century. Holistic thinkers such as Henry More and John Ray wrote about nature from this point of view, as did the renowned Swedish botanist Carl von Linne (or Linnaeus), whose 1749 treatise *The Oeconomy of Nature* popularized the phrase the pre-ecologists favored. In 1793 the Reverend Nicholas Collin asked the American Philosophical Society to support the protection of little-known birds, apparently on the verge of extinction, until naturalists discovered "what part is assigned to them in the oeconomy of nature." God had created the creatures, Collin implied, and for humans to remove them from the natural scheme of things would be both imprudent and irreverent. This line of reasoning forecast the way the ecological perspective would provide an intellectual basis for environmental ethics. The central idea was community membership and its attendant rights.

As a Transcendentalist, Thoreau's holism [theory that entire systems cannot be understood by understanding their parts] stemmed from his belief in the existence of an "Over-soul" or godlike moral force that permeated everything in nature. Using intuition, rather than reason and science, humans could *transcend* physical appearances and perceive "the currents of the Universal Being" binding the world together. Thoreau expressed the resulting perception: "The earth I tread on is not a dead, inert mass; it is a body, has a spirit, is organic and fluid to the influence of its spirit." In this holism, Thoreau professed what might be termed "theological ecology"— God held things together. Still, the scientist in Thoreau emerged every day as he walked the Concord countryside. His journals are crammed with data about how organisms relate to each other and to their environment, and he followed the Linnaean tradition in using the phrase "economy of the universe."

Thoreau's organicism or holism, reinforced by both science and religion, led him to refer to nature and its creatures as his society, transcending the usual human connotation of that term. "I do not," he wrote in his journal for 1857, "consider the other animals brutes in the common sense." He regarded sunfish, plants, skunks, and even stars as fellows and neighbors—members, in other words, of his community. "The woods," he declared during an 1857 camping trip in Maine, "were not tenantless, but choke-full of honest spirits as good as myself any day." There was no hierarchy nor any discrimination in Thoreau's concept of community. "What we call wildness," he wrote in 1859, "is a civilization other than our own." Such ideas are remarkable for their total absence in previous American thought.

Thoreau's Environmental Ethic

Although he did not use the term, an environmental ethic sprang from Thoreau's expanded community consciousness. It began with the axiom that "every creature is better alive than dead, men and moose and pine trees" and went on to question the appropriateness of human domination (kindly or not) over nature. "There is no place for man-worship," he declared in 1852; and later, "The poet says the proper study of mankind is man. I say, study to forget all that; take wider views of the universe." Thoreau's own expanded vision led him to rant against the Concord farmers engaged in the quintessentially American activity of clearing the land of trees and underbrush: "If some are prosecuted for abusing children, others deserve to be prosecuted for maltreating the face of nature committed to their care." Here Thoreau seemed to imply that nature should have legal rights like other oppressed minorities. On another occasion, he pointed out the inconsistency of the president of an anti-slavery society wearing a beaver-skin coat.

While Thoreau avoided the word "rights," his association of abused nature with abused people placed him squarely in the path that the new environmentalists would later follow. But in the middle of the nineteenth century, Thoreau was not only unprecedented in these ideas, he was virtually alone in holding them. In fact, it is likely that no more than a handful of Americans even read these iconoclastic journal entries until the first complete edition of Thoreau's unpublished work in 1906. Of course Henry Salt, Thoreau's first biographer, knew about them, but Salt's perspective, as noted, was English. He would have at least partially understood what Thoreau meant about muskrats being his brothers.

Social Issues in Literature

CHAPTER 2

Walden and the Environment

Walden Was Written as New Englanders Systematically Destroyed Their Forests

Ted Steinberg

Ted Steinberg is a professor of history and law at Case Western Reserve University. His books include Acts of God: The Unnatural History of Natural Disaster in America, Slide Mountain; or, The Folly of Owning Nature, *and* Nature Incorporated.

According to Steinberg, as Henry David Thoreau sought an escape from New England life by going to Walden Pond, New England was in the midst of a two-hundred-year war on the woods, during which vast areas of forest were cut down. In tracing the history of this "war," Steinberg shows how New Englanders, seeking to make the American landscape more like Europe's, as well as to replace the natural ecosystem with an agroecosystem capable of feeding an ever-growing population, systematically cleared away forests. Steinberg notes that Thoreau's death in 1862 coincided with an end to the destruction of New England forests, as many farmers migrated farther west. But the new forests that grew back lacked the old forests' rich diversity of trees, and the New England woodlands would never be the same.

In 1845, nature writer Henry David Thoreau, seeking to escape the hustle and bustle of daily life, went looking for a quiet little piece of land free from the intrusions of New England's thriving agricultural economy. Ironically, he had to settle for an old woodlot in Concord, Massachusetts, a place where farmers routinely ventured to find fuel to heat their homes. One of the nineteenth century's leading critics of progress and its impact on the natural world, Thoreau came of age in a region thoroughly transformed by human action, a place of fields and fences so devoid of forest and animal habitat that the largest mammal commonly encountered was the muskrat.

A Battle with the Natural World

In Concord, near the legendary Walden Pond, Thoreau built himself a cabin and lived in it for about two years. The journal he kept while there formed the basis for his most famous book, *Walden; or, Life in the Woods.* "When I first paddled a boat on Walden," he wrote, "it was completely surrounded by thick and lofty pine and oak woods." Relishing that fond memory, he continues: "But since I left those shores the wood-choppers have still further laid them waste, and now for many a year there will be no more rambling through the aisles of the wood, with occasional vistas through which you see the water. My Muse may be excused if she is silent henceforth. How can you expect the birds to sing when their groves are cut down?" At roughly the time that Thoreau headed to Walden, some 60 percent of the New England landscape had been converted from forest into open fields, almost the exact opposite of today, where the reverse ratio of forest to open space prevails. The incessant cutting of trees to create new farmland and supply households with fuel drove Thoreau to distraction. As he put it: "Thank God, they cannot cut down the clouds."

The domesticated countryside Thoreau confronted was the product of endless hours spent cutting down trees, planting fields, and tending fences, as the colonists and their descendants entered into battle with the earth and its ecosystems. In simple terms, an ecosystem is a collection of plants, animals, and nonliving things all interacting with one another in a particular locale. Left undisturbed by humankind, the New England landscape would eventually revert largely to inedible woody matter, to forest. Ecosystems in such "climax" states contain only small quantities of human food. Agriculture tries to stop nature from evolving toward this food-scarce condition and instead guides the land into yielding a supply of crops suitable for human consumption. Tillers of the soil seek to turn the landscape into an agroecosystem, a collection of domesticated plants for feeding people. Farming is always a battle with the natural world, a struggle to keep nature from doing what comes naturally.

How did the landscape Thoreau sought to escape come to be? What kinds of threats emerged to stymie farmers in their quest to simplify the region's diverse set of habitats? What was gained and lost, ecologically speaking, as the woods, to paraphrase Thoreau, went prematurely bald?

From Forests to Fields

When the colonists arrived in New England, forest was the dominant form of vegetative cover. It was the main obstacle standing between them and their quest to remake the region into an agricultural utopia. Initially, the Europeans went in search of cleared areas suitable for planting crops, appropriating Indian fields and thereby saving themselves from the backbreaking labor involved in clearing forestland. Plymouth and many other New England towns, for instance, were established on old Indian fields. One early settler was even confident that enough "void ground" existed in New England to serve the short-term needs of all those who chose to venture overseas.

Eventually, however, population growth outstripped the supply of Indian land, forcing the European settlers to cut down more forest themselves. For most of the colonists, cleared, arable land was the landscape most familiar to them from life back across the ocean. It took time to become accustomed to the hard labor involved in cutting down the woods. In the northern colonies, trees were usually chopped down, al-

WALDEN;

OR,

LIFE IN THE WOODS.

By HENRY D. THOREAU,

AUTHOR OF "A WEEK ON THE CONCORD AND MERRIMACK RIVERS."

I do not propose to write an ode to dejection, but to brag as lustily as chanticleer in the morning, standing on his roost, if only to wake my neighbors up. — Page 92.

Copy 2

BOSTON:

Henry David Thoreau's Walden, *first published in 1854, called for environmental awareness during a 200-year campaign by New Englanders to systematically replace forests with farmland.* © Historical/Corbis.

though sometimes a technique known as girdling was used. Girdling, a practice far more common in the South, involved cutting a horizontal channel all the way around the tree, which stopped the vertical flow of sap. Deprived of sap, the leaves would die and the branches eventually fell off, leaving the surrounding land dry and suitable for planting.

New Englanders, however, generally clear-cut the forest, in part because the demand for fuel wood and lumber encouraged it. The market for potash, an alkaline substance that came from burning hardwood trees, also drove farmers to cut and burn the woods with a vengeance. Used to manufacture soap, glass, and gunpowder and to bleach linens and print calicoes, potash served a range of industrial uses but at the expense of farms, which lost the nutrients that the ashes would otherwise have released back into the soil had they not been exported to market.

With their very existence dependent on the successful production of food, farmers had little if any time for removing stumps and stones. Instead, they adapted to the half-cleared fields by planting Indian corn (maize) and grass; both grew well in such an environment. A pattern of "extensive" farming began to emerge. Rather than carefully tending arable land, engaging in crop rotation, manuring, and the thorough removal of stumps and stones—all recognized as part of proper agricultural practice in Europe—New England farmers simply exploited the soil and then forged ahead with the clearing of new land. Cutting down trees remained hard work, but it was easier to partially clear the land, plant it, and then move on to another small plot than to constantly improve the soil on one field to the high Old World standards. The colonists were too busy figuring out how to produce food rapidly to worry about efficient agricultural practices. Disheveled-looking their fields may well have been—indeed, many travelers commented on the rather sorry shape of the colonial landscape—but they were also serviceable and well adapted to surviving in a new, land-rich environment.

Early on, the colonists adopted the Indian practice of planting corn along with beans and pumpkins or squash. These plants reinforced one another, resulting in high agricultural yields. The stalks of corn facilitated the growth of beans by giving them a structure to climb. The beans, as noted earlier, replenished the nitrogen that the corn drained out of the soil, bolstering fertility. And the pumpkins were a valuable source of food in the pioneer environment. "All kind of garden fruits grow very well," wrote Puritan Edward Johnson in 1654, "and let no man make a jest at pumpkins, for with this fruit the Lord was pleased to feed his people to their good content, till corn and cattle were increased." After a few seasons, however, the colonists slowly began the process of transforming New England into an image of the Old World, planting European grains such as wheat and rye alongside the maize, a crop they never abandoned in part because it proved a more reliable source of food. . . .

Pests and Diseases

As the colonists remade New England into a replica of the Old World landscape, abandoning corn, beans, and squash for fields planted with European wheat and rye, they ran into trouble. Passenger pigeons posed an early threat. Known to fly in flocks ranging in number from hundreds of thousands to millions—reportedly taking hours to travel by and leaving dung several inches thick on the forest floor—the birds descended in droves on grain fields. In 1642, the pigeons attacked grain in a number of Massachusetts towns. They also fed on the acorns and chestnuts in the surrounding forest, driving the settlers' hogs (set free to feed in the woods) to the brink of starvation.

Native species of insects also found the new sources of plant food a major attraction. So many grasshoppers converged on the grain crops of the first Massachusetts settlements that the colonists were reportedly forced to use brooms to sweep them into the ocean. In 1646, caterpillars swarmed the region, becoming fairly regular visitors to the colonists' grain fields in the ensuing years. The Indian practice of burning the land held down these insect populations. But with the Native Americans largely driven from the land and the prospect of a brand new source of concentrated food—the wheat and rye—insect populations reached new heights.

Livestock too was threatened, especially by wolves. It took only a decade after the Pilgrims first arrived for a bounty to be placed on the gray wolf, with all the colonies eventually following suit. Sometimes especially rapacious animals might elicit stronger measures. In 1657, New Haven, Connecticut, posted a sum of five pounds for anyone who could kill "one great black woolfe of a more than ordinarie bigness, which is like to be more fierce and bould than the rest, and so occasions the more hurt."

Some of the threats to agriculture were of the colonists' own making. A fungus known as the black stem rust (or "blast") proved devastating to rye and especially wheat. When the colonists brought barberries from Europe to North America to make jam, they also imported, unwittingly, this fungal parasite that used the barberry as a host. In the eighteenth century, a number of New England states passed laws aimed at eliminating barberry bushes, but with penalties rarely assessed, their effect remains open to question. The blast proved so insidious that in some areas of New England it came close to completely annihilating the wheat crop.

By arresting forest growth and replacing it with an abridged form of plant life, the New England colonists found themselves locked in a battle with various pests and diseases. Simplifying nature had its costs. Sustaining this streamlined agroecosystem required the input of a great deal of human energy—whether that meant sweeping insects into the sea or pursuing wolves through the forest—to achieve the desired results.

Too Many People

Even if pests and disease could be fended off, there was still the threat posed by too many people pressing against a limited resource base. In much the way that the British economist Thomas Malthus (1766–1834) would later outline, population began to outstrip New England's land supply as early as the 1720s. This trend, combined with an economic slump that began at the outset of the century, presented a serious challenge to the farm economy.

The Malthusian crunch hit the older towns of eastern Massachusetts first. As population expanded against the limits of a finite supply of land, these settlements became more crowded. Inheritance customs added to the problem. Typically the eldest son received a double share of the estate left by the deceased; the remaining shares were divided evenly between both sons and daughters. During the first few generations, the division of land in this way still allowed each succeeding generation a sizable enough piece of property to operate a successful farm. But as the eighteenth century unfolded, the repeated division led to progressively smaller estates. In the 1600s, land holdings commonly ranged between 200 and 300 acres; by the second half of the 1700s, farm size plummeted to the point where the average holding may have been as small as only 40 to 60 acres. Reverend Samuel Chandler of Andover, Massachusetts, who had seven boys to take care of, wrote in the 1740s of being "much distressed for land for my children." Relentless population pressure also forced up the price of land in older towns outside of Boston, such as Concord and Dedham, Massachusetts. Malthusian pressures may even have compelled New Englanders to rethink their views on inheritance. By the 1720s, some Massachusetts farms were being passed down intact to the oldest son, with the other siblings left to either migrate or find some other means of support. America, the land of opportunity, was in trouble.

The ecological effects of the rise in population are difficult to pin down. Some historians have blamed the population and land imbalance for soil exhaustion and a consequent lowering of agricultural production. New England agriculture was beginning to unravel. Increasing population and prevailing inheritance patterns ran up against the ecological wall created by worn-out soils. "Patriarchy," historian Carolyn Merchant writes, "had come into conflict with ecology." But whether the declining yields stemmed from soil exhaustion or some other factor is unclear.

Population growth alone does not wear out the soil; certain agricultural practices do. Some historians have argued that New Englanders bankrupted the soil by suspending efforts to recycle nutrients back into it. They planted year after year but failed to properly use the manure necessary to keep the soil in good shape. Colonial farmers remained wedded to an extensive mentality—looking for new fields instead of improving the yields of the ones they had—that kept them from employing any of the basic reforms necessary for ecologically sustainable agriculture. Inefficient farming meant declining soils and falling agricultural yields, a pattern made all the worse by population growth.

A more satisfying interpretation of New England's demographic dilemma and its ecological consequences emerges when we focus on natural hay meadows—the heart of the region's agriculture. Meadowland provided a vital source of food for livestock and, through the manure the animals generated, a nutrient boost for the soil. Farming under this system required just the right amount of land suitable for crops, livestock, and hay. Achieving the correct balance between these various types of land uses held the key to putting agriculture on a solid ecological footing. When the demographic crunch emerged in the eighteenth century, it made life for the younger generation difficult in at least one major respect. It now became harder for them to gain access to the right configuration of landed resources, that is, cropland, pasture, and especially meadowland. Soil exhaustion, per se, may not have been the main problem in Concord and other older New England towns, places where farmers lived and died by the availability of natural meadows. Access to meadowland and marsh grass attracted the early colonists and contributed to the birth and longevity of these settlements. Perhaps it can explain their downfall as well. When population pressure and inheritance customs made meadowland inaccessible to increasing numbers of young farmers, the diversified basis of the agroecological system suffered. America's experiment as the land of opportunity foundered on the limits of meadow grass.

Into this distressing and delicate social and ecological context marched the British with their challenge to the autonomy of the 13 colonies. On four occasions between 1764 and 1773, Parliament asserted its right to tax the Americans, with the last attempt ending in the famous Boston Tea Party. Land pressures alone did not cause the colonies to break with Britain, but they certainly provided a context that made Parliament's attempt to subordinate the colonies all that more intolerable. That Concord, Massachusetts, a town buffeted by the changes outlined here, would serve as the starting point of the American Revolution was no accident. . . .

A New, Simplified Forest

Thoreau's death in 1862 corresponded with the end of the story that had been unfolding in New England for over two centuries. By the 1860s, the region's long-standing battle to conquer the forest was coming to a close as farmers migrated out of the region to richer soils in the Midwest. Trees began to encroach on the abandoned farmland. But it was a unique new forest environment that developed. The oaks, hickories, and chestnuts that had carpeted southern New England when the colonists arrived did not return right away. A new kind of forest arose, one composed of tree species adapted to life in a landscape filled with fields. It was a simplified woodland, made up largely of white pine trees, a drought-tolerant species with seeds easily dispersed by the wind. The reincarnation of New England as a white pine region was an artifact of its earlier creation as a land of fields and farms.

As the war against the woods ended, a new front in the struggle with nature was beginning to open. Thoreau lamented many aspects of what agriculture had done to New England but saved his greatest ire for the factories and railroads that soon intruded on the landscape. And yet, how ironic that this critic of progress should have earned a living as a surveyor, measuring the land into discrete parcels so it could be bought and sold. Indeed, he had surveyed Walden Woods so extensively that he once wrote, "I now see it mapped in my mind's eye ... as so many men's wood lots." When he lugged his surveying equipment out to mark off the land, he participated in what became a major preoccupation for nineteenth-century Americans: the transformation of the earth—its soil, trees, and even water—into a set of commodities.

Humanity's Love of the Wilderness Is a Recent Development

Stephen Budiansky

Stephen Budiansky is a historian, writer, and journalist. He is the author of a number of books on military and intelligence history, science, and the natural world, including The Covenant of the Wild: Why Animals Chose Domestication *and* The Bloody Shirt: Terror After Appomattox.

Budiansky places Henry David Thoreau's love of nature in its cultural context, showing how humans' love of wildness in nature is a fairly recent historical development. Budiansky explains that, for centuries, humans loathed or feared untamed nature, but with the advent of romanticism and transcendentalism, a cult of the wild sprang up, in which Thoreau plays a central role. Thoreau did not love the wild as an end in itself, Budiansky asserts, but as an escape from the travails of village life and the artificiality that he came to detest. Since Thoreau's time, the love of nature for its own sake has become a given among environmentalists, but according to Budiansky this appreciation of nature has taken its own artificial and absurd turns.

How have we come to believe things about nature that are so untrue? Young love always has a dash of infatuation, and our love for nature is young indeed.

In 1653 the English historian Edward Johnson took pen in hand to tell the world of the untamed forests of North America, so unlike anything that European settlers and travelers had known from the Old World. A "remote, rocky, barren, bushy, wild-woody wilderness," he called it. He did not mean it as a compliment.

The modern-day admiration of nature is so nearly universal that it comes as a shock to discover of what recent vintage these feelings are. For all but the last two hundred years of civilization, anyone expressing a conviction that wilderness contained anything admirable, much less that it was the embodiment of perfection, would have been considered eccentric, if not insane. Before the end of the eighteenth century, mountains were universally disliked. They were "warts," "wens," "the rubbish of creation," places of desolation suitable only, as in Dante's *Divine Comedy*, to guard the gates of hell. Dr. Johnson [English lexicographer and writer Samuel Johnson], in 1738, expressed the opinion that the Scottish hills "had been dismissed by nature from her care." Other seventeenth- and early eighteenth-century writers were no less contemptuous of the wild. The Alps were "high and hideous," "monstrous excrescences of nature," the place where nature had "swept up the rubbish of the earth to clear the plains of Lombardy." An early visitor to Pike's Peak wrote, "The dreariness of the desolate peak itself scarcely dissipates the dismal spell, for you stand in a confusion of dull stones piled upon each other in odious ugliness."[1] . . .

For the wilderness had long been viewed by most people with hostility for perfectly good reason. Mountains were places of wolves, bears, bandits, bad roads, and violent and unpredictable weather. The North American forests harbored wild animals and hostile Indians. To a farmer who needed to clear fields to feed his family and graze his livestock, the woods were a backbreaking obstacle; felling trees and pulling stumps was the most arduous job a settler faced. [As historian Roderick Nash has noted.] It was only "the literary gentleman wield-

1. Ronald Reese, "The Taste for Mountain Scenery," *History Today*, vol. 25, 1975: 305–312.

ing a pen, not the pioneer with an axe" who could think otherwise. To this day, farmers are not conspicuous among the backpacking set. . . .

When Henry David Thoreau wrote, "in wilderness is the preservation of the world" he was not talking about the role of tropical biodiversity in maintaining the life-support processes of the planet. By "the world," he meant the world of man—specifically the spiritual world of man. Nature mattered, not for its own sake, but for what it could do for man's soul. "I derive more of my subsistence from the swamps which surround my native town than from the cultivated gardens in the village," he went on to explain. "My spirits infallibly rise in proportion to the outward dreariness. . . . When I would recreate myself I seek the darkest wood, the thickest and most interminable and, to the citizen, most dismal swamp. I enter a swamp as a sacred place,—a sanctum sanctorum." His motive was a "desire to bathe my head in atmospheres unknown to my feet."

Here is where so much of the mischief begins. Thoreau's declaration that "in wilderness is the preservation of the world" is one of the most quoted in modern environmental writing. It is always interpreted as a precocious ecological insight, anticipating by a century the modern recognition of the environmental damage that pollution and development are wreaking. Few people recognize the fundamentally religious motivation that Thoreau's words gave voice to.

Thoreau's Escape to Walden

For Thoreau, nature's chief value was that it was not the town. The woods were an escape from social corruption, or, more to the point, people. "Society is always diseased, and the best is the most so," he wrote in *The Natural History of Massachusetts*. The conventions of social intercourse were stultifying [absurd] "Politics . . . are but as the cigar-smoke of a man." Commerce was frivolous. Labor was degrading, farming no better than serfdom. Even man's amusements were nothing but a sign of the depths of his despair. "The greater part of what my neighbors call good I believe in my soul to be bad." The word *village*, he said, comes from the same Latin root as *vile* and *villain*, which "suggests what kind of degeneracy villagers are liable to." Thoreau wanted to "shake off the village," where men spent empty, monotonous, vacuous, and spiritually impoverished lives. "I confess that I am astonished at the power of endurance, to say nothing of the moral insensibility, of my neighbors who confine themselves to shops and offices the whole day for weeks and months, aye, and years almost together," he wrote. It was the freedom that nature had to offer that was its chief attraction. Thoreau went to live at Walden Pond, he said, "to transact some private business with the fewest obstacles."

If nature's value rested upon its being a refuge from the evils of society, then nature, by definition, meant separation, the absence of man. It was the very fact that man and all his follies were not to be found there that made nature estimable. What Thoreau disliked about man's presence was not that it would interfere with or degrade critical biological processes; what he disliked about man's presence was its presence. Thoreau disapproved of wealth, church, rules, voting, dinner parties, and young men not as smart as he who sought to join him on his walks. He would tell the last that he "had no walks to throw away on company." The link between environmentalism and escapism is an enduring one, and Thoreau's admiration of the wild as a place to turn one's back on the town can be heard in the words of David Brower, Bill McKibben, and other nature writers of our day.

Thoreau's aversion to society (and to holding down a regular job) readily explains some of the appeal that the woods held for him. But nature's stock was rising at this time for other reasons, too—all just as far removed from anything to do with ecological science, wildlife conservation, biodiversity, or the other concerns that modern environmentalists try to graft upon the woodsy philosophy of Thoreau and his fellow travelers. Many of the early American nature worshipers, including Thoreau's fellow townsmen in Concord [American transcendentalist philosopher and essayist] Ralph Waldo Emerson and [American transcendentalist writer] Amos Bronson Alcott, were deeply revolved in a whole laundry list of reform-minded causes that all shared an antipathy to the corrupt social status quo. Temperance, the abolition of slavery, dietary reform, and alternative medicine may not seem at first glance to have much in common, but all were a rejection of evils that man appeared to have brought upon himself—and all saw salvation, spiritual and physical, in a return to nature. Just as "natural law" had shown the falseness of monarchy, slavery, and other political systems that denied men their God-given rights, so natural foods and natural healing would show the falseness of alcohol and artificial medicines that denied men their God-given health.

The Water Cure

This was an age of revivalism, millenarianism [the idea that there will be a great transformation in society], and utopianism, brimming with enthusiastic schemes for remaking the world. One scheme that managed to roll together several of these enthusiasms in one, with virtuous and uncorrupted nature at its core, was the "cold water" movement. Publications extolling the multiple virtues of cold water flourished in the early and mid-nineteenth century. *Water-Cure World; Water-Cure Journal; The Magnetic and Cold Water Guide* were but a few of many. The Hutchinson Family Singers, a musical family from New Hampshire whom one historian has called America's first pop singing group, took to the road in the 1840s with a homespun message blending denunciations of slavery, war, alcohol, doctors, tobacco, and the usurpation of Indian lands with paeans of praise to water:

Oh! If you would preserve your
health

And trouble never borrow,

Just take the morning shower bath,

'Twill drive away all sorrow.

And then instead of drinking rum,

As doth the poor besotter;

For health, long life, and happiness,

Drink nothing but cold water.

Yes, water'll cure most every ill,

'Tis proved without assumption;

Dyspepsia, gout, and fevers, too,

And sometimes old consumption.

Your head-aches, side-aches, and
heart-aches too,

Which often cause great slaughter;

Can all be cured by drinking oft

And bathing in cold water.

It was only later that temperance became the special do-
main of little old ladies and busybodies; in the early nineteenth century excessive alcohol consumption was a major social ill in America, and the temperance cause attracted broad
support from the reform-minded intelligentsia. Skepticism
about the cures offered by contemporary medical science was
equally well founded in reality; it was not until the very end
of the nineteenth century that a patient seeking the assistance
of a medical doctor was more likely to be improved than
harmed by the treatment prescribed. Most of the cures consisted of violent purging and vomiting, bleeding, blistering,
and the liberal application of remedies containing opium and

alcohol or, with an alarming frequency, slow-acting poisons such as mercury and arsenic. A particularly favored cure-all was calomel, or mercurous chloride, a powerful purgative—as well as a central nervous system poison. It almost certainly hastened the demise of many in those days, including, in 1799, George Washington, who fell ill with a cold, was thoroughly dosed by his attending physicians, and promptly dropped dead. (Calomel was singled out for special excoriation in another of the Hutchinson Family's songs: "And when I must resign my breath, / Pray let me die a natural death, / And bid the world a long farewell, / Without one dose of Calomel.")

The Return to Nature

But the urge to look to nature for the answer went much further. Cold water was not just a wholesome substitute for intoxicating liquors; it was God's answer to man's ills. "The God of nature has never made—at least for the globe we inhabit—any other drink but water," extolled William Alcott, the physician cousin of Bronson. "Let us . . . abandon Satan's system of poisoning . . . and adopt God's system, based on truth—on the harmonies and congenialities of nature," wrote another water enthusiast. "Wash, and be healed," said yet another. This was more than a temperance campaign. This was the stirring of a new religion. Illness was the result of violating nature's laws. Good health could be obtained only by restoring harmony and balance. Spiritual health and physical health were inseparable, and both were linked to obedience to the lessons that nature taught, as a reflection of God's plan. Rather than try to rise above nature and the "brute" or "animal" instincts, as Christianity had so long seemed to urge, the message of these "Christian physiologists" was that man must give up the sinful luxuries and excesses of civilization and return to nature. Nature was not the fallen world of fleshly and unclean desires; it was the pure and uncorrupted creation of God. "Alas! the beast that roams the forest . . . may boast of greater consistency, of a more implicit obedience to the laws of Nature, and Nature's God, than proud Man!" declared an article in one of the many publications devoted to the ideas of Samuel Thomson, a nineteenth-century herbalist whose *New Guide to Health* had sold one hundred thousand copies. "Those who live in the nearest state of nature, also approach the nearest state of perfect health." (Another reformer of this era who achieved contemporary fame marching an army of followers back to nature was Sylvester Graham, mostly remembered today only for the cracker that bears his name. Graham was an immensely popular preacher of the new gospel of salvation through hygiene; he blamed "crowded cities" for the ruin of the human family, and urged a return to that state of primeval simplicity "when man was free from disease, and a perfect stranger to vice." Graham preached a regimen that eschewed all "artificial stimuli" in favor of cold baths, fresh air, exercise, loose-fitting clothing, and a diet of nothing but coarse rye or wheat meal, hominy, and pure water.)

The new doctrine of dietary salvation that Graham and Thomson were offering up to their mainly Yankee audiences struck many familiar chords, with its emphasis on self-denial and Puritanism as the pathway to the kingdom of heaven. The Graham system of living was, like Christianity itself, a means to a higher spiritual end. True to the evangelical spirit of Graham's message, followers of the Graham diet offered up testimonials telling of the "flood of light" they experienced once they began eating coarse bread and taking icy baths. Indeed, some of the health-cure preachers who came to fame in the mid-nineteenth century ventured to suggest that eating right would not only unstop the bowels but bring the millennium [a thousand years of peace ruled by Jesus Christ].

Nature Worship

In worshiping nature as God's creation, these nineteenth century nature enthusiasts forged another link between the love of nature and the beliefs in its perfection and its possession of an innate purpose apart from man's. Thoreau was surely speaking tongue in cheek when he and a few fellow dropouts from Concord society formed the Walden Pond Society as an alternative church for Sunday morning meetings and proposed plucking and eating wild huckleberries as a substitute for the more conventional sacrament of communion. But there was no hint of irony in Emerson's transcendental conviction that nature was the literal dwelling place of God: "The aspect of nature is devout. Like the figure of Jesus, she stands with bended head, and hands folded upon the breast. The happiest man is he who learns from nature the lesson of worship." Emerson believed that nature was both a source of moral instruction and discipline and the holy of holies where man would become "part or particle of God" himself.

This was but a prelude to the nature worship of [nineteenth-century naturalist] John Muir, who was to become far and away the most successful popularizer of the cult of the wild. The son of a stern Scottish Presbyterian turned Disciple of Christ, Muir brought the full force of his evangelical upbringing to his devotion to nature. His father was a thoroughgoing disciplinarian who discouraged any reading but the Bible and ordered the family to bed promptly after 8 P.M. prayers. He once set John to work for months on end digging a ninety-foot-deep well with nothing but hammer and chisel; he would be lowered in a basket in the morning and hauled up in the evening. Finally, at the age of thirty, Muir had had enough and, abandoning the family's Wisconsin farmstead, set out to walk to the Gulf of Mexico by "the leafiest and least trodden way" he could find.

Yet even as he rebelled, he could not shake his evangelical roots. Feeling the beauty of nature, he said, was to experience "a glorious conversion." Discovering Twenty Hill Hollow near Yosemite was "a resurrection day." The forests were "temples," trees were "psalm-singing," natural objects were "sparks of the Divine Soul." In the wild, indeed only in the wild, could one "touch naked God" and "be filled with the Holy Ghost." Once, climbing a mountain, he slipped and nearly fell but was touched by a "blessed light" and saved; "had I been borne aloft upon wings, my deliverance could not have been more complete." Such a nature religion was incomplete without nature evangelism: "Heaven knows that John the Baptist was not more eager to get all his fellow sinners into the Jordan than I to baptize all of mine in the beauty of God's mountains," he wrote in his journals.

Unlike Thoreau, Muir does not in the least appear to be joking about his version of the communion sacrament:

> Do behold the King in his glory, King Sequoia. Behold! Behold! seems all I can say. Some time ago I left all for Sequoia: have been & am at his feet fasting & praying for light, for is he not the greatest light in the woods; in the world. I'm in the woods woods woods, & they are in me-ee-ee. The King tree & me have sworn eternal love—sworn it without swearing & I've taken the sacrament with Douglass Squirrell drank Sequoia wine Sequoia blood, & with its rosy purple drops I am writing this woody gospel letter.... I wish I was so drunk & Sequoical that I could preach the green brown woods to all the juiceless world, descending from his divine wilderness like a John the Baptist eating Douglass Squirrels & wild honey or wild anything, crying, Repent for the Kingdom of Sequoia is at hand.... Come Suck Sequoia & be saved.

Even in his arguably more sober moments Muir's religion was unwavering. Nature was a place to find God; nature *was* God. As God was perfect and pure, so nature was perfect and pure. There is "perfect harmony in all things here," he wrote; nature is the "pure and sure and universal," the "Song of God, sounding on forever."

Modern Implications of Nature Worship

This sentiment survives virtually unchanged among the nature lovers of our day. Asked by the Canadian environmentalist Farley Mowat how they came to devote their lives to environmental protection, one activist after another described a "conversion" experience. Mowat himself told how he "glimpsed another and quite magical world—a world of Oneness." All the more so because it did not include people: "When I came back from the Second World War, I was so appalled by the behaviour of modern man that I fled to the Arctic to escape him," Mowat wrote. "The world of non-human life became for me a sanctuary."

Such feelings toward nature are real and earnest and genuine. Thoreau and Muir struck a deep chord that resonates yet. Those who fight for more wilderness areas these days will speak of experiencing a sense of connection with something greater than themselves, something "primeval, threatening, and free of jarring reminders of civilization"; the defenders of the deer talk of feeling "close to nature" when they come across one of these wild animals in an urban park; even Harvard biologist and environmental advocate Edward O. Wilson punctuates 350 pages on biodiversity with the argument that it should be preserved because "wilderness settles peace on the soul." But none of this is a very good measure of what constitutes ecologically sound, or even ecologically feasible, policy. Religion answers a genuine human emotion, but it is not science. And even the most ascetic religion of salvation is not very far removed from self-indulgence, with all of the attendant dangers of that emotion. It is just too easy to mistake one's personal feelings of exaltation for some universal truth. Virtuous self-indulgence has been a foible of those who have been seeking salvation in nature from Thoreau's day to ours.

There are fewer true ascetics about these days; today's nature lover is more likely to try to save the rain forests by buying the correct brand of chocolate-and-nut-covered ice-cream bar than he is to try to save his soul by eating nothing but coarse flour for two years. But attitudes toward conservation practice remain entangled in a web of introspective human sensations—the aesthetic love for nature's beauty, the spiritual search for solitude and peace and personal health, the nostalgic yearnings for a golden age.

Thoreau's Nature Was an Artificial Construct

Wright Morris

Wright Morris was an American novelist, essayist, and photographer known for his works about the people and artifacts of the Great Plains. Among his books are The Field of Vision *and* Plains Song: For Female Voices, *both of which won National Book Awards.*

According to Wright Morris, in Walden *Thoreau's art is greater than his argument. Tapping into America's desire for escapism, or "flight," Thoreau creates a myth that he himself did not live out. Morris contends that Americans' love of nature was not new with Thoreau, but he gave it civilized respectability. Yet Thoreau himself did not flee to nature; he went toward places and facts, not from them. Thoreau left Walden to pursue other business but left no similar record of those pursuits. He said that his business was being a "saunterer," but according to Morris the true American saunterer is to be found in another of Ralph Waldo Emerson's followers, Walt Whitman.*

I went to the woods because I wished to live deliberately, to front only the essential facts of life, and see if I could not learn what it had to teach, and not, when I came to die, discover that I had not lived.

This statement, by one of the world's free men, has captivated and enslaved millions. It is a classic utterance, made with such art that what is not said seems nonexistent, civilization and its ways a mere web of *in*essentials, distracting man from the essential facts of life. The texture of this language and the grain of this thought are one and the same. To fall under its spell is to be in possession of *one* essential self. A sympathetic mind may find the call irresistible. The essential facts of life will seem to be these facts, all others but stratagems, snares, and delusions, although the facts to support such a conclusion are not self-evident. They are implied, but implied with such persuasion they seem facts. That is Thoreau's intention. But his art is greater than his argument. Although he sought to persuade through *facts*, through the testimony of the raw material, it is his craft as a writer that gives his facts conviction, and his example such power. It is his art, not his facts, that sent his readers to the woods.

America's Natural State of Mind

As [French writer] André Malraux points out in *The Creative Act*, the artist is launched on his career not by the supremely beautiful face, but by the supremely beautiful painting. It is not just the Woods, but *Thoreau's Woods*, that captivate us. What he chooses to give us is so patently essential—to the picture he is painting—and what he withholds is so plainly inessential, we feel, to life. It is all a matter of selection. Of art, that is.

The American mind, the Yankee imagination, had sap and substance before this man spoke, but I believe we can say it had no grain until Thoreau. It is the natural grain of this mind that still shapes our own. The self-induced captivity of the American mind to some concept of Nature—NATURE writ large—can be traced, it would seem, to the shores of Walden Pond. Here is the first contour map of what we might call our *natural* state of mind.

With his customary intuition concerning things American, [English novelist] D.H. Lawrence, in his *Studies in Classical American Literature*, points this out.

NATURE.

I wish I could write it larger than that.

NATURE.

Benjamin [Franklin] overlooked NATURE. But the French Crèvecoeur spotted it long before Thoreau and Emerson worked it up. Absolutely the safest thing to get your emotional reactions over is NATURE.

The unmistakable accuracy of this barb makes us wince. Nature—even Nature tooth and claw—is child's play when confronted with *human* nature. The problem reduced to its essentials, is NATURE v. Human Nature. It was this problem that led Thoreau to take to the woods. But he would not have been led there—he more or less tells us—if he had not believed that taking to the woods was the prevailing tendency of his countrymen.

Thoreau Made Nature Respectable

In *Walden* that prevailing tendency received its classical form. Back to Nature was not new with Thoreau—it had, in fact, lost the gloss Crèvecoeur gave it—but Thoreau endowed it with a civilized respectability. The romantic wash of color is replaced with the essential facts. But the result—since he was an artist—was to heighten the romantic effect. Through the sharp eyes of this capital realist, NATURE, writ large, looked even more inviting, and the realistic myth took precedence over the romantic one. It remains, to this day, a characteristic quality of the American wilderness.

Flight from something, we can say without quibbling, was foreign to Thoreau's mind, and we know that when he turned his back on the city it was *toward* the facts—not away from them. In his own mind he was facing the very facts that his friends and neighbors turned away from, and it is this sentiment, not a romanticized Nature, that gives *Walden* its power. But in a culture of cities, as the country was then becoming, this sentiment went against the very grain of culture, and became, in time, a deliberate rejection of the essential facts of this culture.

In 1845, when Thoreau went to Walden, he had a continental wilderness lying, *before* him, and he was hardly in a position to see that he had actually turned his back on the future. Or that the prevailing tendency of Americans was *flight*. Flight, not from what they had found, but from what they had created—the very culture of cities they had labored to establish.

Each of these cultural centers, each of these established towns, became a fragment of Europe and a past to get away from—the prevailing tendency of Americans being what it was. Thoreau did not expose this tendency to examination—he accepted it. It satisfied, after all, the drift and grain of his own mind. He *began* at that point—in a language and a tone similar to that which informed the Declaration of Independence. He established, as that document sought to, certain inalienable human rights. One of them being to take to the woods, if and when you felt the need.

The Lure of Nature Survives Conflicting Facts

The principle of turning one's back on unpleasant facts—unpleasant because they were so deeply inessential, so foreign, in a way, to our essential Nature—is one *naturally* congenial to the American mind. Thoreau gave this principle its classic utterance. In his spirit, if not in his name, we still take to such woods as we can find. If his genius had been of another kind he might have scrutinized this principle, rather than Nature, but it was his destiny to be the archetypal American. To put, that is, the prevailing tendency to a rigorous test. That he did; that he did and found it wanting, since he both went to the woods and then left them, is an instructive example of how a necessary myth will survive the conflicting facts. The wilderness is now gone, a culture of cities now surrounds us, but the prevailing tendency of Thoreau's countrymen—his more gifted countrymen—is still to withdraw into a private wilderness.

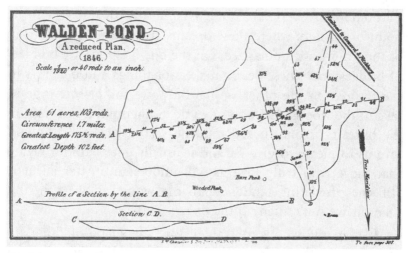

Hand-drawn map of Walden Pond.

William Faulkner is the latest [in the 1950s], but he will not be the last, to pitch his wigwam in the pine-scented woods.

If other American classics have been more widely read— and as a rule they would be children's classics—none has left such an impression where it counts the most: on impressionable men. In Thoreau they see the archetypal *man* as well as the American. He is our first provincial with this universal mind. Under the spell of his style his raw material, that little piece of it around Walden Pond, was processed into a universal fact. There it stands, like an act of Nature, having little to do with the man who made it, and, as so often happens, we henceforth have little to do with him. He walks off—he seems to pass like the seasons—leaving us with his pond. With all those facts, essential and inessential, gleaming like a scimitar [a curved, single-edged sword] in the sun, not to mention the problems that his stay in the woods did not resolve.

For Thoreau, Walden Was Not Enough

We have his word for it that Walden was not enough. Is another life of quiet, *very* quiet, desperation all that lies in store? The rest is silence. There is nothing for us to do but go to Walden and see for ourselves.

Somewhere between Walden Pond and Boston—at some point of tension, where these dreams cross—the schizoid soul of the American is polarized. On the one hand we are builders of bridges and cities, we are makers of things and believers in the future. On the other we have a powerful, *private* urge to take to the woods, as we so often do. Sometimes a note left on the bureau, or one tucked into the vest, asks those who still love us to please forgive us, and it usually goes without saying that those who truly love us will understand. After all, it is still the prevailing tendency. To the woods, if we can find them; if we *can't*, then, to the dogs.

It is in the woods at Walden that the shape of things to come is formulated. Here the American mind is divided down its center, fact against fact. At the threshold of our literature the prevailing tendency is given its classic statement and justification. Turn your back on the city, the civilized inessential, and withdraw into the wilderness. Turn your back on those things built with hands, and withdraw into a world not made with hands. The territory ahead lies behind you. *Allons donc!* [Therefore go!] Take to the woods.

There Is No Explanation of Why Thoreau Left Walden

What we have is Nature, NATURE writ large. But it was Thoreau who was the first to remind us that men lead lives of quiet desperation, and another year at Walden, we have reason to believe, he would have been leading one of them. But after two years he had had it. He left the woods, he tells us, for as good a reason as he went there. We have to take that on credit, however, since he does not tell us how it worked out. There is no equally reassuring volume on the world he went back to. Walden was an experiment, he says, and what he learned from it was this: that if a man advances confidently in the direction of his dreams, and endeavors to actually live the life he has imagined, he will meet with a success unexpected in the common hours.

To that we can say *Good!* So he says, and so we believe. But in what direction, pray, now led his dreams? We know only that they led him into the wilderness, not out of it. He does not trouble to tell us in what way his prevailing tendency reversed itself, or, if it did not, how and why it lost its efficacy. No other tendency, of equal inspiration, took its place. Having entered upon and completed his experiment, Thoreau then took eight years to formulate his report, and it stands as the central experiment of his life. And yet we know he went on living. We even know he went on writing. But neither his living nor his writing found another center, another *tendency*, that engaged him like the one that took him to the woods. We might say that having finished with that experiment, he had finished with his life. There is more day to dawn, he reassures us, but he is silent on what day it might be, and in our hearts we feel that the man we know is still in the woods.

What Is Thoreau's Business?

What *kind* of man was he? Any number of men, most of them distinguished, have added their touches to his self-portrait. They reaffirm, rather than rearrange, the classical lines. Emerson likened the taking of his arm to the taking of a piece of wood. It would be sound, grainy wood. The elbow honed and polished like the handle of a cane.

But in the main the self-portrait is more than enough. He would ask us to face him as he himself sought to face the facts.

> If you stand right fronting and face to face to a fact, you will see the sun glimmer on both its surfaces, as if it were a cimeter, and feel its sweet edge dividing you through the heart and marrow, and so you will happily conclude your mortal career. Be it life or death, we crave only reality. If we are really dying, let us hear the rattle in our throat and feel the cold in the extremities; if we are alive, let us go about our business.

What business? Ah, there's the rub. Not any ordinary business, certainly, since he has just told you, in no uncertain terms, that in nine chances out of ten your *business* is killing you off. It is why you are dying. It is why, as you read him, he has the ring of truth. It is why the essential facts seem to be that we must go to the woods ourselves if we are to live deep and suck the marrow out of life. It is our busy-ness—if we want to face the facts—that is killing us.

This unexamined paradox is one of many that Thoreau leaves with the reader—forever leaves with him, that is, since a volume on that subject never appeared. *Walden*, like *Huckleberry Finn*, is a *beginning*—the opening chapter of a life, a story, one that enthralls us, but with all the remaining chapters missing.

A capital realist, the archetypal honest man, when Thoreau had had enough of the woods he left them—but the facts of his life among men are neither essential nor reassuring. What *could* follow on such a beginning? Deep in our hearts we know that the best has been lived, that we have now had it, which is why we don't ask, why we will settle for a pond, a raft, and Huck Finn.

Behind all this talk about facts, and fine talk it is, one fact escapes comment. There is no other business; no other essential business. One leaves the pond to disappear, like an echo, into the wings. The curtain comes down. The lights come on. Can that be the end? It can't—but those are all the facts we are going to get. In the beginning, and a very unforgettable beginning it was, a man went deliberately into the woods. We know that for a fact. But there is very little evidence, of the same order, that he ever came out.

> I should not talk about myself so much [he tells us] if there were anybody else whom I knew as well. Unfortunately I am confined to this by the narrowness of my experience.

The revelation of this statement may lead us to overlook its accuracy. The narrowness of his experience is one of the essential facts in his book. I am not concerned with the absence of those things that we now exploit. On such matters as women and sex we can respect his silence. What he chooses to tell us is much more to the point. The insights of Freud—imaginative in nature—have made it difficult, if not impossible, to face the facts of an age different from our own. I would like to suggest that the myth of Nature—writ large, as Thoreau wrote it—can be as overwhelming, traumatic in fact, as the myth of Sex. It is the myth of Nature that concerns us in Thoreau. He turned to Nature as D.H. Lawrence *turned* to Sex, and both transformed what they saw, what they found, to suit the needs of their genius and their temperament. It is difficult to say which offers the greater handicap. Each man sees, in the mirror of his choice, what he is compelled to see. For all of the material details, the counting of nails and beans, Walden Pond is a mythic, personal vision, and in its depths lurk such facts as it is the genius of the beholder to see. It is on the same map, and no other, as Huck Finn's mighty river, and its memorable facts are the product of the same chemistry, the poet's imagination processing the raw-material facts.

Whitman, Not Thoreau, Is America's True Saunterer

If we now ask Thoreau about his own *business*, he will give us a curious answer. His true profession was, he would have us know, a "saunterer." If this word has a strong romantic coloration—we *see* Thoreau in the woods, but we do not see him saunter—it is still consistent with his role in the myth. The busy man has no time to saunter. In fact, he has no place. One saunters in Nature, plucking a leaf, chewing a twig. It is the saunterer who stops and asks in amazement, "What is the grass?" [a reference to Walt Whitman] It is the saunterer who has the time to tell you that it is the flag of his disposition, or better yet, the beautiful uncut hair of the graves. It is the saunterer who leans and loafs at his ease. And with that picture, that telling self-portrait, we know, in our bones, that Thoreau was no saunterer. We know only, thanks to his statement, that he wanted to be. But I believe it no accident, however, that the archetypal saunterer of our dreams, like the archetypal Nature man, Thoreau, began precisely at the point where Thoreau left off. The prevailing tendency, having finished with Thoreau, reappears as a sauntering Song in Walt Whitman, as he makes his way, idly, down the endlessly open road. Walt Whitman, a Kosmos, of Manhattan the son, is that other half of the Nature picture, but this time it is Human Nature—and Walt Whitman's own. Turbulent, fleshy, sensual, eating, drinking, and breeding, Walt Whitman wants space, he wants air, he wants OUT!

Unscrew the locks from the doors!

Unscrew the doors themselves from the jambs!

In theory, if not in practice, in private, if not in public, this was, and still is, the prevailing tendency of his countrymen.

Thoreau's Walden Was Never Environmentally Pristine

Robert Sattelmeyer

Robert Sattelmeyer teaches in Georgia State University's Depart-ment of English and is the author of numerous articles on Henry David Thoreau, Mark Twain, and Ralph Waldo Emerson.

Behind Henry David Thoreau's carefully constructed image of Walden Pond in the 1840s lies the reality that it was not, at the time, the pristine wilderness that it seems in the book. Thoreau clues the reader in to this reality, but does so subtly enough that many readers may miss his implication that, as Sattelmeyer writes, the community surrounding the pond was little more than a "rural slum." Ironically, Walden Pond had been bought by Emerson for its lumber, Sattelmeyer points out, and the area had fewer trees in 1840 than it has had before or since. Refores-tation and Walden's *influence have since brought the forest back. But, as Sattelmeyer explains, the Walden Pond of Thoreau's book is more of a virtual image than a snapshot of reality.*

Like the raft on which Huck Finn and Jim float the Missis-sippi River, Thoreau's cabin at Walden Pond has come to possess a kind of hyper-canonical status as cultural icon, both temporary homes figuring a confluence of self and place that suggests an ideal if unattainable American existence for the individual in harmony with nature. While the raft is clearly a fictional device that ferries its inhabitants from one adventure to another, punctuated by brief intervals of idyllic drift, Walden Pond and its surrounding forests are clearly more rooted in reality. The pond is, after all, an actual place, and the historical Henry Thoreau did live there in a cabin of

Robert Sattelmeyer, *Thoreau's Sense of Place: Essays in American Environmental Writ-ing.* Iowa City: University of Iowa Press, 2000. Copyright © 2000 by the University of Iowa Press. All rights reserved. Reproduced by permission.

(mostly) his own making during a fourteen-month period from 1845 to 1847. Every few years someone attempts to duplicate Huck and Jim's raft trip and gets written up in the local papers, but their numbers pale in comparison to the tens of thousands who annually make what [Harvard professor] Lawrence Buell has aptly termed "The Thoreauvian Pilgrimage" to Walden Pond. This disproportion exists not just because Walden Pond is easily accessible by car (unless you're trying to visit on a warm summer weekend). It exists because Walden is not only a literary shrine but also a cultural site that provides a focal point for a series of environmental concerns and beliefs that continue to be central to our collective social life a hundred and fifty years after Thoreau moved back to town.

Walden's Image

Central to these concerns is the image of Walden's pristine and isolated nature, an image both fixed and celebrated by Thoreau's book. This image, in turn, has helped define the controversies of recent years over development of areas adjacent to the pond, and also helped define the extension of the idea of the site to include what is called "Walden Woods"—the pond's watershed as well as the pond itself. The image remains fixed even in the name of a prominent local organization devoted to preservation of the pond and its environs, Walden Forever Wild. Powerful (and productive) as this concept is, however, it tends to obscure and distort both the actual nature of Walden Pond and its surrounding land features during the 1840s and 1850s, and Thoreau's actual portrayal of it in *Walden*.

Thanks to Buell's recent study, *The Environmental Imagination*, we have a thoughtful and comprehensive account of the successive possessions and repossessions of Thoreau and Walden Pond by disciples, publishers, literary scholars, environmentalists, and the public. An important corollary to this story is how Thoreau himself engineered the origins of what Buell terms the "will to pastoralize Walden" by transforming a busy commercial and agricultural site with a long and complex history of human settlement into a remote forest lake that impressed him (and later readers) "like a tarn high up on the side of a mountain." This part of the story is rather difficult to tell, for it requires that we try to look at *Walden* without the accumulated weight of nearly a century and a half of reception by critics and general readers alike. We cannot help being influenced by its reputation as a critique of industrializing America and its celebration of the narrator's solitary life in the woods. But we can situate the image of Walden that we have inherited against what we can discover and infer about the actual environs of Walden during this period, and we can also examine some of the unsettling information about the pond and its surroundings that Thoreau himself provides in the text and in his Journal.

Thoreau's Complex Information

The information that Thoreau himself provides should come as no surprise to careful readers of *Walden*, for it is axiomatic [evident without proof] that Thoreau almost always qualifies if he does not outrightly subvert what appear to be his dearest formulations. Indeed, the seemingly endless power of semination [cultivation] that the text seems to possess owes a great deal to the fact that its most cherished wisdoms seem to be always already undercut. This feature seems counterintuitive at first, going against the grain not only of *Walden*'s canonization as a scripture of individualism, iconoclasm, and environmental correctness, but also its announced rhetorical drive toward clarity and simplicity ("I went to the woods because I wished to live deliberately," etc.). But, as anyone knows who has tried to teach *Walden* to undergraduates, clarity and simplicity are not really prominent features of the text. "It is a ridiculous demand," Thoreau says in the "Conclusion," "which

England and America make, that you shall speak so that they can understand you," and he seems more often than not bent on demonstrating his allegiance to this belief. To take perhaps the most obvious example of his persistent subversion of a simple understanding, Thoreau concludes "Economy," the longest and most polemical chapter of *Walden* and the chapter in which he describes his "less is more" philosophy, with a poem by [English poet] Thomas Carew titled "The Pretensions of Poverty." This poem begins:

Thou dost presume too much,
poor needy wretch,

To claim a station in the firmament

Because thy humble cottage, or thy
tub,

Nurses some lazy or pedantic virtue

In the cheap sunshine or by shady
springs,

With roots and pot-herbs.

Clearly, if one actually reads this strategically placed counterpoint, it undercuts the mode of life that Thoreau has just described, undermines his claim to authority, and emphasizes that the author, whatever rural virtues he may practice, possesses a highly refined literary sensibility which he exploits in highly self-conscious ways, using both the pastor [idealizing rural life] and anti-pastoral traditions to erect his own edifice of words. In a similar vein within "Economy," Thoreau the radical simplifier, after describing in great detail his spartan [practicing self-denial] diet, seems to subvert the entire experiment by concluding, "The reader will perceive that I am treating the subject rather from an economic than a dietetic point of view, and he will not venture to put my abstemiousness [moderation in eating and drinking] to the test unless he has a well-stocked larder." Even within the list of foodstuffs it-self, the careful reader will notice that about two-thirds of the items listed are marked by a bracket denoting "All experiments which failed." Throughout the book, readers who take Thoreau's ringing formulations too literally may find them-selves in the position of the traveler who is the butt of the boy's joke in the "Conclusion." Assured by the boy that the bog he is about to walk his horse into has a hard bottom, he advances confidently in the direction of his dreams, only to find his horse mired to its girth. "'I thought you said that this bog had a hard bottom.' 'So it has,' answered the latter, 'but you have not got halfway to it yet.'"

Undercutting the Image

Armed with this cautionary tale, it is not unreasonable to look for evidence in the text itself that the relative remoteness and natural forested beauty of Walden Pond—the overwhelming image that readers and pilgrims carry with them—are perhaps not all that they were cracked up to be. In fact, in the course of his fable, Thoreau both constructs and deconstructs this image of remote beauty, playing on the reader's desire in much the same way that his equally canny New England de-scendant Robert Frost does in "The Road Not Taken," estab-lishing the unshakable image of a road less traveled when there really was none. ("Though as for that the passing there / Had worn them really about the same, / And both that morn-ing equally lay / In leaves no step had trodden black.") Not surprisingly, much of the evidence about what Walden Pond and Walden Woods were actually like when Thoreau was liv-ing there is to be found in one of the shortest and arguably the most anomalous chapter in the book, "Former Inhabit-ants; and Winter Visitors."

"Former Inhabitants," because its subject and tone seem so out of keeping with the rest of the book, is one of the least noticed sections of *Walden*. Conventionally, it could be said to occupy a place in the book's narrative of triumphal emergence as a kind of meditative lull preceding the rebirth of spring. In like manner, the second half of the chapter, "Winter Visitors," records the paucity [insufficient amount] of human contact that the narrator experienced at this season, containing flattering portraits of the improvident [American transcendentalist writer] Bronson Alcott and [American transcendentalist poet] Ellery Channing, a curt dismissal of Emerson, and concluding with the narrator waiting for "the Visitor who never comes." More importantly, though, "Former Inhabitants" opens a window on aspects of local culture that tend to be bracketed off in the rest of the book. This window is small, and open only briefly, but it can alter one's experience of the book in the same way that a consideration of Carew's poem (rather than the conventional skipping over) alters "Economy."

A Rural Slum

"Former Inhabitants" provides a glimpse of Walden's social past, the harshness of which is muted by the chapter's oddly discordant elegiac tone—discordant not only because a brusque disregard of the past is more characteristic of the book's tone, but also because there was not much about the lives of the people described to be nostalgic or elegiac about. But what is most surprising about the chapter is that it describes the area around Thoreau's cabin—a mile from any neighbor, as we recall—as prominently marked by the remains of a small, straggling village that had until rather recently occupied the spot, home to a group of people that readers don't tend to associate with Walden Pond. Cato Ingraham, for example, a slave, lived across the road. He had a grove of walnut trees, but "a younger and whiter speculator got them at last." There was also Zilpha, another African American who had a little house and spun linen for the townsfolk: "She led a hard life, and somewhat inhumane," Thoreau says with uncharacteristic understatement. Brister Freeman, yet another slave, tended an apple orchard and lived down the road toward town. Across the road was the Stratton family homestead, their orchards abandoned and reverting to forest. Near this was Breed's location, once the site of a tavern. The Breed family was destroyed by a demon, Thoreau says, a demon "who has acted a prominent and astounding part in our New England Life"—rum. Then there was Wyman the potter, who squatted in the woods quite near Thoreau's cabin, so poor that when the sheriff came to collect unpaid taxes there was nothing even to confiscate. Finally, the most recent occupant of the neighborhood before Thoreau was Hugh Quoil, an Irishman, an ex-soldier who may have fought at Waterloo. He too was an alcoholic. Thoreau sometimes encountered him in the woods, wrapped in a greatcoat in midsummer, shaking with delirium tremens. He died in the middle of the road that runs by Walden during the first year Thoreau lived there. These people were "universally a thirsty race," Thoreau says, and used the pure waters of Walden Pond only to dilute their rum.

Reminded as we frequently are today of issues of race and class, and of the tendency of previous literary histories to ignore the darker underside of American life and canonical texts, it should not be altogether surprising to find that Thoreau's cabin was constructed amid the remains of what was essentially a rural slum, a small village of outcasts, misfits, and derelicts who were excluded from the more homogenous society of Concord. Even today, the landfill and the trailer park that were until recently in operation across the road from Walden extend this heritage of class exclusion to the area. In Thoreau's day, the residents were slaves, ex-slaves, alcoholics, rum sellers, and the Irish, people who were literally marginalized and pushed out of Concord proper.

Perhaps the reason for readers' and critics' general failure to pay much attention to this aspect of *Walden* comes from Thoreau's practice of cloaking these stories of exploitation, exclusion, self-destruction, and economic failure in a fog of sentimental elegy in the manner of [English novelist Oliver] Goldsmith or [English poet Thomas] Gray. Here is the conclusion of his meditation on the cellar holes of these former residents:

> Still grows the vivacious lilac a generation after the door lintel and the sill are gone, unfolding its sweet-scented flowers each spring, to be plucked by the musing traveler, planted and tended once by children's hands, in front-yard plots,—now standing by wall-sides in retired pastures, and giving place to new-rising forests,—the last of that stirp, sole survivor of that family. Little did the dusky children think that the puny slip with its two eyes only, which they stuck in the ground in the shadow of the house and daily watered, would root itself so, and outlive them, and house itself in the rear that shaded it, and grown man's garden and orchard, and tell their story faintly to the lone wanderer a half century after they had grown up and died,—blossoming as fair, and smelling as sweet, as in that first spring. I mark its still tender, civil, cheerful, lilac colors.

Raymond Williams observes, in *The Country and the City*, speaking of one of Thoreau's models here, Gray's "Elegy in a Country Churchyard," that the musing poet cannot really have it both ways: he cannot both praise the luck of those who lived in the "cool, sequestered vale," *and* bemoan the repression of the "chill penury" that stifled their lives. Similarly, Thoreau ought not to be able to have his rhetorical cake and eat it too, both disclosing the conditions that led to the displacement or extermination of these people—racism, economic exploitation, prejudice against immigrants, and the pandemic abuse of alcohol in the early nineteenth century—while at the same time deriving a tender poetic melancholy from the lilacs blooming around their cellar holes. But he does. And that may be one reason why readers generally fail to take in fully the implications of "Former Inhabitants."

A Virtual Isolation

Once the recent human history of Walden Pond is established through "Former Inhabitants," other less consecutive bits of information in the text may be adduced [used as evidence] to elaborate its social dimensions. For not only was it the site of a village just recently failed, but also the current site of rather intense commercial and agricultural activity. For example, we learn that during the winter of 1846–47 the pond was harvested for ice, not just by local landlords but in a large-scale operation that involved more than a hundred men and heavy equipment who arrived daily by train from Cambridge. Although Thoreau says that during the winter "no wanderer ventured near my house for a week or a fortnight for a time," reinforcing the portrait of his self-sufficient isolation, the fact that more than a hundred men with heavy equipment were at work every day in front of his house suggests a somewhat different reality, and reinforces the notion that Thoreau's isolation was a virtual and an imaginative rather than an actual one.

Moreover, the fact that these laborers arrived daily by train underscores the fact that the completion of the railroad to Concord in 1844—the year before Thoreau moved to Walden—brought the village more solidly into the economic orbit and labor market of Boston. The railroad touches the pond just a few hundred yards from the site of Thoreau's cabin, and passes within earshot of the site of the cabin itself; so that living there in the 1840s must have been rather like living near a just-completed freeway today, only with more intermittent noise. The shanties of the Irish laborers who built the railroad still dotted the right-of-way, and could still be found, inhabited, near where the tracks met the pond. Thus, Thoreau's initial claim that he lived "a mile from any neighbor" is true only if we exclude the Irish, who were not only "silent poor" but apparently invisible poor as well. In a Journal entry for July 11, 1851, Thoreau comments on the Irish and the smell of their shanties along the railroad as he walked near the pond, but in the world of *Walden* they are unremarked except for the exemplary shanties of James Collins, which Thoreau tore down for building material, and that of John Field, which he visited in "Baker Farm."

Emerson's Woodlot

As for the pristine character of Walden Pond and its surroundings, it needs to be recalled that Concord was the first inland town the English established, in 1635. Thus, the area had been subject to pressures of settlement and cultivation and environmental change by Europeans and their descendants for over two hundred years by the time Thoreau moved to the pond. The landscape of Concord in the 1840s and 1850s was an agricultural one, dominated by tillage and pastures and cutover areas, with only about 10 percent of the area in forest. In fact, 1850 was the historic low point of forest coverage in Concord: it had been steadily decreasing since initial settlement, and has been increasing steadily ever since, as agricultural lands were abandoned and gradually reverted to forest. This decline was also true, although to a lesser extent, of the area around Walden Pond. Here and there the text of *Walden* provides clues to this fact, though the overwhelming impression one is left with is of a lake surrounded by forest. But increasingly the actual landscape consisted largely of fields, such as that eleven-acre plot that Thoreau used a part of to grow his beans on, and woodlots, utilized and managed by the farmers and the townspeople for firewood, both for their own consumption and as a cash crop to sell on the Boston market. The site of Thoreau's cabin was a plot of land recently purchased by Emerson for a woodlot, and the "tall arrowy white pines, still in their youth" that he cut for the timbers of his cabin had doubtless seeded there by wind dispersion after the area had been cut over at some earlier time. Much of the wooded land that did exist in Concord was coppice woods, second-growth timber created by allowing trees to resprout from stumps, a practice which yielded a quick growth of wood suitable for fuel. The landscape of Walden in the mind's eye derives from Thoreau's memory: "When I first paddled a boat on Walden, it was completely surrounded by thick and lofty pine and oak woods"; whereas the actuality, grudgingly acknowledged in a late revision, is that "But since I left those shores the woodchoppers have still further laid them waste, and now for many a year there will be no more rambling through the aisles of the wood."

Nor was the prevalence of open lands solely due to the advent of European axes and plows. Native Americans of southern New England had traditionally set fires to create open savannas richer in game and more conducive to successful hunting than old-growth forests, and they used fires to create crop fields, too. The "ashes of unchronicled nations" that Thoreau disturbs with his hoe in "The Bean Field" are reminders of the long history of both fire and agriculture in the area around Walden.

A Dynamic Environment

A physical as well as a literary archaeology of the site of Thoreau's experiment—the Walden Pond of the book and the Walden Pond State Reservation of today—discloses a richly varied human and natural environment that closely mirrors economic, agricultural, and demographic developments in Concord. Like all natural environments, it was and is a dynamic and not a static system. It had been used for more than two hundred years by the descendants of European settlers, and before that for thousands of years by Native Americans, perhaps as long ago as its emergence from the retreating ice sheet. At the time of Thoreau's residence there in the 1840s, it was under particularly intense pressures of cultivation and development from the ice trade, the railroad, and the heavy demand for wood for fuel. As elsewhere in New England, agricultural use around Walden was already beginning to decline, and when the demand for firewood waned after the Civil War, the area joined the rest of the region in the gradual reversion of pastures and cropland to forest. Despite today's pressures of urban sprawl and development, the area around the pond is significantly more heavily wooded today than it was when Thoreau was creating its image as a remote forested lake. Thanks both to reforestation and the power of *Walden's* rhetoric, today's Walden Pond resembles the Walden Pond of the book more than the actual Walden Pond of 1845 did.

At the same time, the area had a rich if problematic human history, one which exposes aspects of Concord culture largely invisible or present only in abstract critiques in the book, things like the legacy of slavery in Massachusetts, the unsettling influx of large numbers of immigrants, and the prevalence of alcoholism in New England.

A Public Pond

Walden Pond was not, in short, either a retired or a pristine place; in fact, one could hardly have chosen a more visible and public spot to retire to in the environs of Concord, for the pond had always had a close connection with the town. But this fact merely highlights the publicness if not the publicity of the gesture of moving there in the first place, which Thoreau had discussed with Ellery Channing and perhaps Emerson the previous year. When Thoreau moved to the pond, he already had in mind some literary project based on the experiment, for he started a new journal volume devoted to recording and immediately working up his experiences there right from the beginning. No doubt he conceived his experiment knowing that it would invite comparison with the other experimental communities, such as nearby Brook Farm [a utopian experiment in communal living] and Fruitlands [a utopian agrarian community], which had sprouted during the 1840s. And it echoed self-consciously the pioneering fever of the country itself, its rush to Oregon and California. The against-the-grain quality of the experiment (Man Builds Log Cabin in Walden Woods) was actually good copy, and led to a brief burst of notoriety when, on the basis of his lectures about life at the pond, he was written about, attacked, and defended in Horace Greeley's *New York Tribune* over a period of several weeks in 1849. It is against all these contexts that Thoreau's paean [praise] to solitude and simplicity and nature must be seen. As for Walden itself, it can't really be Walden Forever Wild because it was never really wild to begin with. But despite the pressures of swimmers, picnickers, and pilgrims, its watershed in some ways is less intensively exploited today than it was one hundred and fifty years ago. Finally, the Walden Pond of the book, it must be said, is a carefully constructed literary site, less Thoreau's home than his home page, a virtual space he designed to represent himself and to promote his business, even if it was only listening to what was in the wind.

Walden Displays Thoreau's Growing Environmental Consciousness

Lawrence Buell

Lawrence Buell is a professor at Harvard University. He is a specialist in early American literature and a pioneer of ecocriticism, the study of literature and the natural environment. He is the author of Literary Transcendentalism, New England Literary Culture, *and* The Future of Environmental Criticism.

For Buell, Walden *is not Henry David Thoreau's most self-conscious environmental statement. The fruition of his ideas about nature is to be found in subsequent works. But Buell notes that the seven successive drafts of* Walden *as well as the progress of the final revision display Thoreau struggling unevenly toward an understanding of humanity's place in the natural world.* Walden *itself shows a movement away from homocentricity (centered around man) toward ecocentricity (centered around the environment) that suggests Thoreau's own movement away from self and toward nature. As the story of Thoreau's stay at Walden Pond unfolds, it shows the gradual unfolding of Thoreau's environmental consciousness.*

Thoreau is the patron saint of American environmental writing. This eminence did not come easily to him. For more than a generation after his death, he remained obscure; and in his relatively short life he had to struggle to arrive at the deep understanding of nature for which he is now remembered. Indeed, Thoreau spent his entire career laboriously trying to sort out the competing claims of nature and

Lawrence Buell, *The Environmental Imagination: Thoreau, Nature Writing, and the Formation of American Culture.* Cambridge, MA: The Belknap Press of Harvard University Press, 1995. Copyright © 1995 by the President and Fellows of Harvard College. All rights reserved. Reproduced by permission of Harvard University Press.

culture. It is especially in his partial odyssey from environmental naïveté to comparative enlightenment that he looks most representative of his culture and mirrors most closely today's environmentalist ferment. Thoreau started adult life from a less advantageous position than we sometimes realize, as a village businessman's son of classical education rather than having been versed in nature through intensive botanical study, agriculture, or more than a very ordinary sort of experiential contact with it. Unlike [early American author] William Bartram, he had no man of science for a father; unlike Thomas Jefferson, he had no agrarian roots. From early youth, he enjoyed country rambles, but so did many of his contemporaries. His first intellectual promptings to study and write about nature came from books, school, and literary mentors like Ralph Waldo Emerson. Though he celebrated wildness, his was the wildness not of the moose but of the imported, cultivated escapee from the orchard that he celebrated in his late essay "Wild Apples." His pursuit of nature thus became a fitful, irregular, experimental, although increasingly purposeful self-education in reading landscape and pondering what he found there: a process "of continuously mapping the world and locating the self" thereby. . . .

One of the reasons *Walden* is Thoreau's greatest book is that the transitional struggles of a lifetime are so fully reflected in it. I concentrate on it, therefore, not only because *Walden* remains Thoreau's most enduring work but also because it embeds much of the history of his thinking about the natural environment as it unfolded from his apprentice years to his full maturity. For we should think of *Walden* both as product and as process, a work that took nearly a decade of accumulated experience and revision to complete: the decade that happened to be the most crucial period in Thoreau's inner life.

"The Ponds"

Let us start our examination with a section from the book's central chapter, "The Ponds." Here we see the romantic poet, as he reworked his material from the few simple descriptive paragraphs of his first draft (1846–1847), beginning also to become the natural historian and environmentalist.

In a previous chapter ("The Bean-Field"), Thoreau nostalgically remembers having been first taken to the pond at the age of four, "one of the oldest scenes stamped on my memory." In a pleasing self-indulgent fancy, the speaker goes on to muse that "even I have at length helped to clothe that fabulous landscape of my infant dreams"—referring ostensibly to his bean farming but presumably also to his book. In "The Ponds" however, this reminiscence produces pain. "When I first paddled a boat on Walden, it was completely surrounded by thick and lofty pine and oak woods." He lingers on this memory awhile. "But since I left those shores," he continues, "the woodchoppers have still further laid them waste, and now for many a year there will be no more rambling through the aisles of the woods, with occasional vistas through which you see the water. My Muse may be excused if she is silent henceforth. How can you expect the birds to sing when their groves are cut down?" This is an arresting sequence for several reasons. First, obviously, because the outburst against woodchoppers abruptly halts the kind of nostalgic fantasy indulged just a little earlier. But it also piques our interest because of what it excludes. We are told that the choppers have *still further* laid waste the trees; yet no previous depredations have been mentioned. Perhaps the idyllic mood was so compelling that Thoreau could not bear to mention them, or (more likely, I suspect) Thoreau presumed that his nineteenth-century audience—which in the first instance he imagined as his inquisitive Concord neighbors—would take it for granted that the groves of youth had steadily been thinned. Such was indeed the case: the percentage of woodland in the town of Concord had steadily declined during Thoreau's lifetime, reaching an all-time low of little more than 10 percent almost at the moment Thoreau penned this sentence.

The plot of Walden *coincides with Thoreau's growing awareness of environmentalistm, perhaps motivated by his time at Walden Pond.* © Richard Pasley-Doctor Stock/Science Fiction/Documentary/Corbis.

Thoreau's Shallow Protests

Even more noteworthy, however, is the transience of the speaker's protest. It does proceed for another paragraph, chiefly devoted to complaints about the "devilish Iron Horse" that has "muddied the Boiling Spring with his foot." The speaker looks for a "champion" that will meet the engine "at the Deep Cut and thrust an avenging lance between the ribs of the bloated pest." But this pugnacity dissipates as the next paragraph assures us, "Nevertheless, of all the characters I have known, perhaps Walden wears best, and best preserves its purity." "Rather than directly engaging the realities it displaces," H. Daniel Peck observes, the Thoreauvian "Nevertheless" "deflects them, turns them aslant," smoothing "the temporarily ruffled surface of the pond." A little later on, we are further reassured by the fancy that the railroad workers are somehow refreshed by Walden as the train whisks by: "the engineer does not forget at night, or his nature does not, that he

has beheld this vision of serenity and purity once at least during the day." Thoreau has again transformed Walden back into
a pristine sanctuary.

This sequence dramatizes several important aspects of
Thoreau's naturism. It shows that "thinking like a mountain"
did not come any more naturally to him than it did to [Ameri-
can naturalist] Aldo Leopold, in the famous essay of that title
in which the father of modern environmental ethics confesses
his slow awakening to awareness of the importance of preda-
tors to an ecosystem. Thoreau seems first to have written
Walden without mentioning the history of the abuses suffered
by the Concord landscape, though he was well aware of them.
For example, the Concord and Fitchburg Railroad, laid along
the west end of Walden Pond the year before Thoreau moved
there, was a significant and highly visible cause of regional deforestation, for creating roadways and for fuel. Thoreau knew,
furthermore, that forest conservation had already been advanced as a public concern. In the first section of the *Report
on the Trees and Shrubs Growing Naturally in the Forests of
Massachusetts* (1846), which Thoreau read soon after publication and consulted frequently thereafter, George B. Emerson
had warned that "the axe has made, and is making, wanton
and terrible havoc. The cunning foresight of the Yankee seems
to desert him when he takes the axe in hand." Yet even in the
finished version of "The Ponds," produced amidst recurring
Journal complaints about the philistine obtuseness [ignorance]
of some of the clients for whom he worked as surveyor, Thoreau did not sound the preservationist note loudly. Why?
Probably not because he feared readers would disapprove, but
because the pastoralizing impulse to imagine Walden as an
unspoiled place overrode his fears about its vulnerability to
despoliation. One cannot argue simultaneously that sylvan
utopia can be found within the town limits and that the locale
is being devastated at an appalling rate; and the vision of a
pristine nature close by appealed irresistibly to Thoreau for

personal as well as rhetorical reasons. It was emotionally important to him to believe in Walden as a sanctuary, and it was all the easier for him to do so in the face of contrary evidence because of the myth of nature's inexhaustibleness that mesmerized many of the astutest nineteenth-century minds. If [English poet] Gerard Manley Hopkins, also a preservationist of sorts, could declare near the end of the Victorian era that "nature is never spent," how much easier for Thoreau, writing a generation earlier in a comparatively underdeveloped country, to relieve his chagrin at the local absence of the giant pines he saw being whisked by on railroad cars by thinking, "what a country we have got to back us up that way."

Aesthetics Drives Ethics

Even if Thoreau had stressed the issue of environmental degradation in *Walden*, he might not have opposed it primarily for nature's sake. In the passages we have reviewed, he laments the denuding [stripping] of Walden mainly on grounds of personal taste, as a blow to "My Muse," as ruining the solace of the author's pondside rambles.

Yet the dominance of aesthetic considerations does not imply ethical anesthesia. As Leopold was later to observe in his essay "The Conservation Esthetic," the cultivation of a noncomplacent bonding to nature at the aesthetic level is one of the paths to developing a mature environmental concern. So we should not minimize the potential impact of the challenge the speaker throws out at the chapter's end, when he declares of the ponds, "How much more beautiful than our lives, how much more transparent than our characters, are they! ... Nature has no human inhabitant who appreciates her.... She flourishes most alone, far from the towns where they reside. Talk of heaven! ye disgrace earth." The language here teeters between the old-fashioned jeremiad's [an angry lecture's] familiar call to moral purification and a more pointedly environmental protectionist eviction of fallen humanity from nature. Either way, Thoreau makes the spiritual renewal more closely dependent on nature appreciation than does Emerson, who would never have thought of calling Walden a "character." Finally, Thoreau's pleasing dramatization of the nurturing bond to nature, not only for the nostalgic speaker but even for the inattentive brakeman and engineer, is more likely to reinforce in attentive readers a sense of the rightness of an unsullied nature than to reinforce complacency in the railroad system as an unmixed good.

Moving from Self-Interest to Nature

Since Thoreau, when redrafting *Walden*, added much more to the second half of the book than to the first, it is not surprising that the sorts of alterations we have been considering reflect the changing ratio of homocentrism to ecocentrism as the book progresses. In "Economy," Walden figures chiefly as a good site for an enterprise. Nature is hardly yet present except as a theater for the speaker to exercise his cabin-craft in. Thoreau proceeds for fully one-ninth of the book before providing the merest glimpse of the pond. The section's message of simplification is certainly consistent with an "environmentalist" perspective, as it is for [American romantic novelist] James Fenimore Cooper's Leatherstocking, but Thoreau does not as yet advocate it on this ground, as Natty Bumppo does from the very start of *The Pioneers* (1823). Not until "Higher Laws" does Thoreau restate his philosophy of abstemiousness [restraint] as anything like an environmental ethic, questioning the killing and eating of animals and fish. This slow expansiveness of the sense of moral accountability toward nonhuman creatures is symptomatic. As *Walden* unfolds, the mock-serious discourse of enterprise, which implicitly casts the speaker as the self-creator of his environment, begins to give way to a more ruminative prose in which the speaker appears to be finding himself within his environment. The prose begins to turn significantly in this contemplative direction as it moves from the heroic classicism of "Reading," with its peda-gogical didactics, to "Sounds," where the "language" of "all things and events" impresses itself on the speaker. The text seems at this point to discover, as [Stanford professor] Robert Pogue Harrison beautifully states, that "all that is to be learned about what is real and not real lies in the exteriority of our inner lives." Thoreau's own language helps us put this direc-tional movement of *Walden* in perspective. Earnest struggle partially gives way to receptivity, self-absorption to extrospec-tion. Thoreau's favorite pronoun, "I," appears in the two open-ing chapters an average of 6.6 times per page; in the next six (through "The Village"), 5.5 times per page; in the next five ("The Ponds" through "House-Warming"—the last chapter in which the speaker modifies his environment, through plastering), 5.2; in the final five ("Former Inhabitants" through "Conclusion"), 3.6. Roughly inverse to these figures is his us-age of the following cluster: "Walden," "pond(s)," and the vari-ous nominal and adjectival forms of "wild": once every 1.8 pages for the first two chapters, 1.1 times per page during the next six (through "Village"), 2.3 times per page during the rest of the book.

Geese and Environmental Awareness

These are crude indices. For a more complex understanding of Thoreau's revisionary processes, we must return to the mi-crolevel and examine the use of a single telltale framing de-vice. During the first pondside vignette in "Economy," the speaker devotes a sentence to remembering that "on the 1st of April it rained and melted the ice, and in the early part of the day, which was very foggy, I heard a stray goose groping about over the pond and cackling as if lost, or like the spirit of the fog." An emblematic fowl, forsooth: suggesting both the spirit of nature and the uncertain spirit of the speaker, who has al-ready chronicled his losses in symbolic form (hound, bay horse, turtle dove). The sentence uses the logic of correspondence delicately, evoking it but not depending on it for dogma—true to the uneasy tone of the image. In "Spring," to help draw the year into a symbolic circle Thoreau makes this image return: of "some solitary goose in the foggy mornings, seeking its companion, and still peopling the woods with the sound of a larger life than they could sustain." This passage is actually the second of a two-part series of anecdotes, pursued through several paragraphs, the first of which begins: "I was startled by the *honking* of geese flying low over the woods, like weary travelers getting in late from southern lakes, and indulging at last in unrestrained complaint and mutual consolation. Standing at my door, I could hear the rush of their wings; when, driving toward my house, they suddenly spied my light, and with hushed clamor wheeled and settled in the pond. So I came in, and shut the door, and passed my first spring night in the woods." Thoreau continues by describing the behavior of the "large and tumultuous" flock (he counts them: twenty-nine) as next morning they disport on the pond, then fly off toward Canada, "trusting to break their fast in muddier pools." Then, after brief mention of a duck flock, comes the solitary goose passage. This sequence is significant in several ways. First, it serves as a formal opening and closing device. Second, it confirms the move to a textured and extrospective rendering of the natural world, whose particularity is now so cogent that the exact number of the large flock must be reported. One wonders if Thoreau might have been trying to answer Emerson's challenge in "Literary Ethics" to "go into the forest" and describe the undescribed: "The honking of the wild geese flying by night; the thin note of the companionable titmouse, in the winter day; the fall of swarms of flies, in autumn, from combats high in the air ... the turpentine exuding from the tree;—and indeed any vegetation, any animation, any and all, are alike unattempted." Third, it suggests a recognition of the delicacy of the complementary project to which *Walden* is committed: to turn nature to human uses, as a barometer of and stimulus to the speaker's spiritual development. True, the geese are personified; they seem to participate in a logic of natural symbols: geese returning equals spring, which equals (we soon find, unsurprisingly) spiritual renewal. Yet their materiality is more immediately significant than their symbolism; when they arrive, the speaker goes indoors so as not to scare them. Though they seem to be projections of human desire ("peopling the woods with the sound of a larger life than they could sustain"), the difference between their realm and his is underscored. He provides no quick emblematic fix as he did in "Economy" ("like the spirit of the fog"). The correspondential framework remains implicit, but it is complicated by the facticity [fact] of the waterfowl and the speaker's respect for their interests. This respect is what begins to modulate Thoreau's romantic enthusiasm toward something like environmental awareness in the modern sense.

But the passage complicates the case I have been building for the correlation between *Walden*'s unfolding and the biographical unfolding of Thoreau's own environmental consciousness. For these developments are neither quite linear nor coextensive. . . .

Thoreau's Unfinished Environmental Evolution

To read *Walden* in sequence, bearing in mind the various stages of the manuscript, is to follow this movement through to a certain point in Thoreau's evolution, but not to the end. *Walden* does not contain Thoreau's most self-consciously environmentalist statements, nor his most close-grained nature observations; and its most detailed passages of observation (the description of the ponds and the melting sandbank in "Spring," for instance) are allegorized more aggressively than is typical of Thoreau's later *Journal*. Partly on this account, Sharon Cameron asks us to think of *Walden* as a product got up for public consumption that seriously compromised, if it did not positively betray, Thoreau's deeper quest to fathom nature and his relation to it. That to my mind is to carry a good point (about the *Journal's* intellectual integrity and high seriousness) too far in the right direction and to understate the degree to which the same partial and ragged exploratory questing Cameron ascribes to the *Journal* can be observed at every level of Thoreau's achievement: his life; his journal; the genres in which he wrote for publication; the composition of *Walden, The Maine Woods,* and *Cape Cod*; and the sequential development of all his books. Respecting *Walden* particularly, I believe that its very "failures" enhance its representativeness both as a document of the environmental imagination and as a microcosm of Thoreau's achievement, for he was never able to get beyond an inchoate, fragmentary sketch of his grand effort to comprehend the Concord environment in its multidimensional totality.

Thoreau's Environmentalism Mirrors His Racial Sensitivity

Jeffrey Myers

Jeffrey Myers is an associate professor of English at Manhattan College in Riverdale, New York.

Observers of Henry David Thoreau generally separate his interests in environmentalism and in social justice. They see his refusal to pay his poll tax and his involvement in the Underground Railroad as entirely distinct from his love of nature. Myers suggests that these interests flow out of the same desire for what is right in the world. As opposed to President Thomas Jefferson, who, in European fashion, saw both land and slaves as things to be mastered, Thoreau comes from an entirely different perspective. He is master over neither the land nor another human being, and Myers notes that his attitude toward both nature and slavery evolved for the better over the course of his life and his writings.

A t 5:00 p.m. on October 1, 1851, Henry David Thoreau recorded in his journal that he "put a fugitive slave, who has taken the name of Henry Williams, into the cars for Canada." Certainly the stakes were far higher for Williams, who had eluded capture for more than a year and had bargained, unsuccessfully, with his former "owner" to purchase his own manumission [freedom]. But at that moment the two Henries both risked their freedom: if recaptured, Williams would have been returned, without trial, to his "owner" under Section 6 of the Fugitive Slave Act of 1850; and if caught violating Section 7 of the act, Thoreau would have faced six months in prison and a fine of one thousand dollars. Indeed,

Jeffrey Myers, *Converging Stories: Race, Ecology, and Environmental Justice in American Literature.* Athens: The University of Georgia Press, 2005. Copyright © 2005 by the University of Georgia Press. All rights reserved. Reproduced by permission.

Thoreau notes that he had to wait for the late-afternoon train, because at noon there was a man "at the depot who looked and behaved so much like a Boston policeman that I did not venture that time." Thoreau was frequently a conductor on the Underground Railroad, escorting escaped slaves between Concord and Fitchburg, a countryside that he knew more intimately, perhaps, than anyone of his time. Who better to throw in with, on this stage of the Railroad, than this "surveyor of . . . forest paths and all across-lot routes," who walked for miles over this terrain nearly every day of his adult life?

Thoreau had made it his "business," as he says in *Walden*, to maintain the forest paths, as well as to have "looked after the wild stock of the town [and] watered the wild huckleberry, the sand cherry, and the nettle tree . . . which might have withered else in dry seasons." He goes on ironically to lament that the town "would not . . . make my place a sinecure with a moderate allowance," but I would suggest that his irony is deceptive: Thoreau felt a keen sense of involvement with all aspects of the natural world within the range of his daily walks, an involvement that contained human events such as the fate of a fugitive slave. In this equal involvement with both the human and nonhuman elements of Concord—as habitat, in biological terms, and as local community, in sociological ones—lies the key to Thoreau's movement away from a physiphobic relationship to the Other [Myers defines this as "fear of threat of erasure by the primacy of the natural world"] and his renunciation of ecological and racial hegemony [exertion of control]. Unlike [President Thomas] Jefferson, whose literary reach is continental, totalizing, and imperialist, Thoreau's concern begins with his local environment.

Two Separate Thoreaus

In *The Environmental Imagination*, Lawrence Buell highlights the conflict between critics disposed to see Thoreau as a nature writer and "environmentalist prophet" on the one hand

and those who view him primarily as a "moral reformer" and social radical on the other. There is the Thoreau of "Resistance to Civil Government," "Slavery in Massachusetts," and "A Plea for Captain Brown," who is jailed for his refusal to pay the poll tax and who speaks out against slavery, in defense of John Brown, and against the Mexican American War. Alternatively, there is the "green" Thoreau of *Walden, The Maine Woods*, and "Walking," who engenders American nature writing and environmental activist traditions with his solitude in the woods, his increasingly ecocentric vision of the natural world, and his nascent calls for conservation. Robert Kuhn McGregor, for example, who thoroughly chronicles Thoreau's late-career emphasis on natural history, praises Thoreau's "demand for a life of moral principle," but states that this part of his work "had nothing to do with nature." Len Gougeon treats the development of Thoreau's "commitment to enterprises of social reform" with scant reference to *Walden* and none to Thoreau's nature writing. Thoreau's most recent biographer, Robert D. Richardson, charts Thoreau's "radical positions" toward both politics and nature but treats them as largely separate issues that "balance" one another.

Both groups of critics have done important work in locating Thoreau's influential contributions to social reform on the one hand and environmentalism on the other. But ironically, this bifurcation [two-part split] in critical thinking reproduces the human/nature duality at the root of ecological and racial hegemony, a dualism that Thoreau comes increasingly to distrust. Further, it underscores the difficulty of seeing through this dualism even today, magnifying the intellectual task that Thoreau takes on in the mid-nineteenth century, when such a dualism was taken for granted. Opening a path to a critical examination that reconciles this bifurcation, Buell states that a view of Thoreau that accounts for these seemingly divergent formulations might "overcome the traditional opposition between the 'naturist' and the 'social reformer'" and might show

"how 'private' transactions with nature may be animated, at least in part, by the will to effect transformation of humankind's social identity and indeed the whole fabric of the social."

Ecological Consciousness and Social Justice

My thesis entails a slight emendation [alteration designed to improve] of this insight: I argue that Thoreau's ecological consciousness deeply informs his commitment to social justice— or, perhaps more accurately, that for Thoreau social consciousness and ecological consciousness cannot be separated, just as the human identity cannot be severed from the natural world. These "two" Thoreaus can be reconciled because they are the same Thoreau: the "social reformer" in the Middlesex County Jail and the "naturist" by the shore of Walden Pond stand in the same place, a place that is radically different from Jefferson's materialist objectification of nature and Ralph Waldo Emerson's idealist Transcendentalism. Recently, a number of critics have made a persuasive case for Thoreau as perhaps the first ecocentric thinker, if an imperfect one, in the Euroamerican tradition. I develop my own version of this position by way of demonstrating that the ecocentric vision toward which Thoreau was moving *is* his social justice vision. By repositioning the self in relation to the nonhuman world, Thoreau's ecocentric stance collapses the dualistic human/ nature hierarchy by which land and wildlife are "othered." In doing so, he collapses related hierarchies in the social realm: nature and culture, civilized and savage, white and other. By breaking down the anthropocentric paradigm [centered around humanity] in which humanity occupies a privileged place in the natural world, Thoreau's ecocentricity breaks down the construction of essential differences between races, while at the same time valuing cultural differences. In refusing to exploit nature, Thoreau refuses to exploit other human beings as well. When he questions arbitrarily drawn borders and property lines that fail to acknowledge the organization of ecosystems, Thoreau also questions the economic and political assumptions behind social policies. Thoreau's nature writing and early conservationist ethic are, finally, of a piece with his abolitionism, his developing respect for Native American individuals and cultures, and his opposition to the Mexican-American War.

Central to an understanding of how Thoreau's incipient ecocentricity produces a stance that is both antiracist and environmentalist is what Buell terms the "radical relinquishment [of] . . . individual autonomy itself." The act of self-relinquishment breaks down the separation of the self from the natural world, or rather reveals that separation to be a largely fictional product of modern Western thought, which views the human subject as the telos [center] of the natural world. The Cartesian [after French philosopher René Descartes] tradition that views the human mind as preeminent and the nonhuman world as mechanistic, even ontologically suspect, collapses in the face of a natural world where human beings are not primary, as does the Lockean [after English philosopher John] view of the material world as so much property waiting to be claimed. Even among critics disposed to see Thoreau as the preeminent early environmentalist thinker, there is disagreement over how far he goes in performing such self-relinquishment, if at all. [Professor of environmental studies] H. Daniel Peck, for instance, locates in Thoreau tension between "an endless elaboration of the world through association," a process Peck calls "worlding," and an "equally strong" gesture that would contain the world in "predetermined categories of perception and cognition—to place and organize them, and thereby to know them." However, not only does Thoreau perform such a relinquishment, his relinquishment has ramifications for racial distinction and hierarchy that remain largely unexplored. For if the fiction that human beings are distinct from and superior to the nonhuman world proves to be an unsustainable construct, then the idea that whites are separate from and superior to other races proves equally unsustainable—indeed, the very concept of "race" proves untenable. If the identity of the white subject depends on the mastery over, and ownership of, both land and peoples—as in Jefferson—a worldview that proves the one type of mastery false and oppressive proves the other false and oppressive as well.

Jefferson and Thoreau

Of course, Jefferson and Thoreau have been seen as complementary figures, with Thoreau claiming to extend the Jeffersonian maxim "That government is best which governs least" to "That government is best which governs not at all." Jefferson's obvious sympathy with revolution, his belief that "the spirit of resistance to government is so valuable ... that I wish it always to be kept alive," echoes in the very title of Thoreau's "Resistance to Civil Government." Further, both Jefferson in *Notes on Virginia* and Thoreau in *Walden* write from a sense of place—and in each case involve that sense of place in the development of a philosophy that includes the relationship between democracy and the way people live on the land. Thoreau in his bean field would seem to embody "the American husbandman," "the figure of the American idyll," as Leo Marx puts it, which evokes "Jefferson's idealized portrait of the husbandman, a simple yet educated man, a noble democrat," the repository of "substantial and genuine virtue." ... Both Jefferson and Thoreau would seem to be equally distrustful of the materialistic, mechanized direction of an increasingly commercial American society.

However, a deeper comparison of Jefferson's and Thoreau's engagement with the land and other people, both their literary engagement and their personal interactions, reveals a sharp divide. While both do indeed exhibit a strong sense of place, their sense of self within that place fundamentally differs, with consequences for both race and ecology. Jefferson's sense of place in *Notes on Virginia* emanates from his hilltop mansion, Monticello, which led one visitor admiringly to observe that Jefferson "had placed his mind, as he had done his house, on an elevated situation, from which he might contemplate the universe." Jefferson's placement of his mansion (designed by him, built by slaves) above the natural world that surrounds him contrasts with Thoreau's placement of his simple cabin "by the shore of a small pond . . . in the midst of an extensive wood."

Both Jefferson and Thoreau "may contemplate the universe," but the position from which each contemplates epitomizes the extreme difference between them: the former's "elevated situation" signifies Jefferson's removal of himself from the natural world and his "placement of his mind" outside and above it; Thoreau's situation deep in an "extensive forest" signifies his sense of himself as on an equal plane with the rest of the natural world, contemplating something with which he is interconnected. Jefferson's respect for natural processes does separate him from the Puritan tradition of typology and providential design, but his objectivism is nonetheless productive of a physiphobia nearly as acute as Mather's or Bradford's. This physiphobia is of a piece with his racism, in contrast to Thoreau, whose greater ecological consciousness will lead him to a greater sense of affinity with people of other "races," and even suggest to him the instability of "race" as category in the natural world.

Jefferson's Attitude Toward Land Versus Thoreau's

Jefferson was a farmer who did none of the hard labor of farming: two hundred African American slaves—most of whom Jefferson rarely saw—did all of the agricultural work on Jefferson's eleven thousand acres and built most of Monticello. Thoreau was a farmer who weeded his two and a half acres of beans himself. When Jefferson lived far beyond the means that his slaves could provide, he sold them off to forestall selling parcels of land. Thoreau, when his efforts at "commercial" farming failed, reduced his acreage of beans to a third of an acre, to "live simply, and eat only the crop which he raised." Jefferson's perspective on land and slaves was informed by his belief in the Lockean principles of private property, which allowed Jefferson to consider both human and nonhuman elements of the natural world as, first, separate from himself and, second, as far below him as the valley below Monticello. Thoreau, on the other hand, abjured land ownership, having "in imagination . . . bought all the farms" in Concord but deciding in the end that "a man is rich in proportion to the number of things which he can afford to let alone": he does not believe in land ownership, let alone the ownership of fellow human beings. The two men write from a sense of place, then, but their sense of self in that place fundamentally differs, and in the case of each, his relationship to the natural world mirrors his relationships toward people of color. Thoreau's developing sense of kinship, even of sameness, with animals and even inanimate elements of the natural world—the geese on the pond, the pines that "stand here older than I"—relates to his sense of self-involvement in the fate of African Americans in "Slavery in Massachusetts" and his characterization of Penobscot guide Joseph Polis in *The Maine Woods*. His ecological sense of sameness with things makes the proprietary attitude that Jefferson has toward land and people impossible for Thoreau.

Jefferson and Thoreau "map" not only their immediate surroundings but the West as well. Jefferson's plan for dividing the territory west of the Appalachians in quadrilinear townships was adopted by Congress; he was deeply involved with the map of western Virginia started by his father, Peter Jefferson; and his *Notes Virginia* can be seen as a map and guide for Manifest Destiny [the inevitable expansion of America to the Pacific]. His very conception of how the West would be populated depends on racial categorization and the Lockean doctrine that "ownership" of property can be asserted by occupying and laboring on an "uninhabited" piece of land, justifiable only by considering African Americans and Native Americans as less than fully human. Thoreau of course was also a surveyor of property lines but developed, in his words, into a "surveyor of forest paths and all across-lot routes," which respect no human-drawn property lines. Thoreau ultimately explores a new territory in the relationship of humanity to the rest of the natural world, which requires a remapping of the relationship between groups of people categorized arbitrarily by race. He maps the West as well, but the West that he maps is, as he puts it, "another name for the wild"—and "the preservation of the world" that "wildness" inspires is the territory where ecology and social justice meet.

Thoreau's Changing Attitude Toward Race

Just as there are critics who doubt the ecocentricity of Thoreau, there are those who, quite justifiably, question the thoroughness of his racial egalitarianism. Indeed, his writings often reveal how he operates within the biases of his time, even as he questions them, and he can be maddeningly inconsistent even where he has taken a strong stand against his society's capitalist destructiveness, imperialist ambition, and racial oppression. Tom Lynch has written, for instance, that *The Maine Woods* reveals Thoreau's own nature/culture dualism, that his romantic view of wilderness and American Indians keeps him from understanding the perspective of his Penobscot guides, Joseph Aitteon and Joseph Polis. Jenine Abboushi Dallal locates in "Walking" a sympathy with American expansionism that she attributes to Thoreau's being a disciple of Emerson. Dana D. Nelson highlights the collapsing of slavery into the sufferings of "wage slaves" and an unresolved prejudice against the Irish as part of a masculinist ethic in Thoreau's writings.

But even as these inconsistencies are acknowledged, a number of factors have to be taken into account.

First, Thoreau underwent a remarkable development that for a long time many critics did not fully consider. In the area of natural history, McGregor has demonstrated how Thoreau trained himself as a competent naturalist only in the last decade of his life, after his sojourn at Walden Pond, when "almost by himself," he was "inventing what we call the principle of biocentrism and the science of ecology." "Before 1850," McGregor explains, "Thoreau had written in praise of nature, but only after that date did he begin truly to understand it." Because so much of his writings come almost straight from his journals, composed sometimes years before publication, he allows the reader to see his development in thinking about the natural world in a way that most other writers do not allow. In *The Maine Woods*, for instance, we see Thoreau's thinking about race, culture, and nature mature, without later revision, over a decade that included three separate trips to northern Maine in 1847, 1853, and 1857. We can trace how these three trips influenced and recorded, perhaps even more than his sojourn at Walden Pond, Thoreau's discovery of the source of Euroamerican physiphobia and his renunciation of ecological and racial hegemony. Some of his most famous statements on both civil rights and the natural world come from periods where his thinking was still very much in development. Only by looking at the totality of his work can we see how far his ecocentricity and social justice vision went and how closely connected they are.

Further, in "working with and through," as Buell puts it, "the restraints of Eurocentric, androcentric, and homocentric culture to arrive at an environmentally responsive vision," Thoreau is searching out a position for which there are few models in Western literature. Hence my metaphor of seeking new terrain: in going, intellectually, where few if any Euroamerican writers had gone before, Thoreau inevitably becomes lost, backtracks, retraces his steps, and moves on again. If he never arrives at his destination, that may be because he does not know exactly where he is heading. Yet as he wanders beyond the regions that Jefferson, Emerson, and others have staked out we his readers can trace his path. Thoreau himself rarely makes explicit how his racially egalitarian ethic of social justice fuses with his total ecological consciousness, perhaps because it is obvious to him, perhaps because he cannot see the connection in our contemporary terms. It is up to us to make his connections speak to our current understanding of the social construction of race and the ecological interdependence of humans with the natural world—ideas that were inchoate, in Western literature, in Thoreau's time. Yet even here he gives us intimations of how strongly these ideas were connected in his mind. His statement in "Slavery in Massachusetts" that "Nature has been partner to no Missouri compromise" shows his awareness that racism goes against everything that the natural world tells him about humanity. Finally, even as Thoreau wanders through this territory, he acknowledges, late in his career, that other cultures have better knowledge of it, and that European Americans must learn from other peoples how to coexist with each other and the land.

Thoreau Had an Ambivalent Attitude Toward Hunting

Richard Bridgman

Richard Bridgman taught American literature at Dartmouth College and the University of California, Berkeley. He wrote books on Thoreau, Gertrude Stein, and Mark Twain.

The chapter "Higher Laws" in Walden *is rife with contradictions—more so than any other chapter in the book, according to Bridgman, who contends that Thoreau had particularly conflicted feelings about hunting, a subject that occupied him much during his stay at Walden Pond. Bridgman explains that on one hand, Thoreau could celebrate wildness in his writings to the extent where he envisions eating a woodchuck "raw"; conversely, he could feel abject remorse about the "murder" of woodland creatures.*

"Higher Laws" takes Thoreau more centrally into the wilderness of contradictions that existed in his mind than does any other chapter in *Walden*. Accordingly, it has received much critical attention, generally dedicated to smoothing matters out by tracing a continuous development in Thoreau from the thoughtless savage youth to the reflective adult naturalist. In fact, the confusions of the chapter accurately represent the conflicts in Thoreau caused by the clash of his perceptions with his ideals. Manliness, curiosity, coldness, sympathy, and prudery were all at contest within him.

An Argument for Wildness

The chapter opens with memorable verve. Returning home from another fishing expedition, Thoreau said, he saw a woodchuck "and felt a strange thrill of savage delight, and was strongly tempted to seize and devour him raw; not that I was hungry then, except for that wildness which he represented." This passage is heightened from the original journal entry. The "strange thrill of savage delight" was added, as was the "strongly" that qualifies "tempted." And, giving the woodchuck more identity, its pronoun was changed from "it" to "him." Finally, to "devour him," Thoreau added "raw." And although he had originally commented, "The wildest, most desolate scenes are strangely familiar to me," he prudently excised "most desolate" for publication. Thoreau was not aiming for self-revelation, then, but rather was building an argument on behalf of a wildness of the sort that has proved to be particularly compelling to the urban reader. So elemental is the action of devouring a woodchuck raw, it creates a certain intellectual *frisson* [thrill]. At the same time, it is obviously not to be understood literally, although neither is it a metaphorical act. Rather it is a kind of creative exaggeration, since Thoreau was not talking of a desire to devour a woodchuck raw, but rather of freeing himself of civilized constraints by ingesting the beast's wildness. "Once or twice" while living at the pond, Thoreau remarked, "I found myself ranging the woods, like a half-starved hound, with a strange abandonment, seeking some kind of venison which I might devour."

A Divided Attitude

If Thoreau was preoccupied with carnivorousness, he only practiced imaginary assimilation. In person, his tastes were quite delicate and he abstemious [marked by restraint], especially concerning flesh. In the *Week* [*A Week on the Concord and Merrimack Rivers*], one recalls, he and his brother could not bring themselves to eat the squirrels they had killed, so revolted were they by their skinned bodies. The idea of hunting had its attractions for Thoreau, but its actualities disturbed him. Muskrat hunting in particular gave him numerous shocks: "Yesterday I met Goodwin shooting muskrats and saw the form and blood stains of two through his game-bag. . . . I saw one poor rat lying on the edge of the ice reddened with its blood." Or: "There lies the red carcass of one whose pelt he has taken on the spot, flat on the bloody ice." Or: "We see Goodwin skinning the muskrats he killed . . . leaving their red and mutilated carcasses behind. . . . See the red and black bodies . . . which the crows have already attacked." Throughout his life, the vision of the immediate effects of hunting was understandably repulsive to Thoreau. "What a pitiful business is the fur trade," he told his journal in 1858. "When we see men and boys spend their time shooting and trapping musquash [muskrat] and mink, we cannot but have a poorer opinion of them, unless we thought meanly of them before." Years before, in "Paradise (To Be) Regained," he had declared: "We slander the hyena; man is the fiercest and cruelest animal." If he could not bring himself to cook a skinned squirrel, it was unthinkable that he could literally devour a woodchuck raw.

Yet there were aspects of hunting involving masculine competence that appealed to Thoreau. That is what caused the internal debate in "Higher Laws." Even the hunter whom Thoreau observed year after year slaughtering muskrats and littering the ice with their skinned bodies led Thoreau to observe one day: "Goodwin cannot be a very bad man, he is so cheery." That same winter (1858–1859), Thoreau wrote of the hunters' guns: "I must confess they are to me a springlike and exhilarating sound, like the cock-crowing, though each one may report the death of a musquash." He expanded this idea in revealing ways. "The energy and excitement of the musquash-hunter even, not despairing of life, but keeping the same rank and savage hold on it that his predecessors have for so many generations, while so many are sick and despairing, even this is inspiriting to me."

The Attraction of Hunting

One can see the attraction of hunting for Thoreau: the primitive expression of self in the act of mastery, it is equivalent to life, to energy, to action. Opposed to it is bookish despair, the disease of civilization, of those who live indoors. Thoreau could even find inspiration in the annual slaughter of muskrats because "these deeds of death are . . . evidences of life, for life will still prevail in spite of all accidents." The directness of a Fortinbras [a character in Shakespeare's *Hamlet*] had its attractions, especially if one were not directly confronted with the results of a "rank and savage hold" on life. . . .

Hunting had [other] attractions as well. The same man who could avow that the young man goes to the forest "first as a hunter and fisher, until at last, if he has the seeds of a better life in him, he distinguishes his proper objects, as a poet or naturalist it may be, and leaves the gun and fish-pole behind," *this* man, without any sense of contradiction, could enter this statement in his journal in 1857: "If, as a poet or naturalist, you wish to explore a given neighborhood, go and live in it, *i.e.* get your living in it. Fish in its streams, hunt in its forests." In 1856, Thoreau had made yet another extended justification of hunting, as opposed to mere appreciation of nature. "From the brook in which one lover of nature has never during all his lifetime detected anything larger than a minnow, another extracts a trout that weighs three pounds, or an otter four feet long. How much more game he will see who carries a gun, *i.e.* who goes to see it! Though you roam the woods all your days, you will never see by chance what he sees who goes on purpose to see it. One gets his living by shooting woodcocks; most never see one in their lives."

This might seem a remarkable position for someone to hold who would spend hours seated in a clearing to observe its wild life. But there was always a Thoreau who sympathized with the male mastery connected with hunting. In "Higher Laws," since he was moving toward an argument on behalf of purification of being, Thoreau chose to identify hunting as a stage in one's growth to manhood. As for boys—"*make* them hunters," he counseled, for "we cannot but pity the boy who has never fired a gun." His own youthful callousness was evident in his 1836 review of *The Book of the Seasons.* There, he specified May as "the pleasantest month of the 12," for now "commences the harvest of death." Thoreau then described in a language of comic elevation the young hunters going forth to shoot, until at last a bird was brought down, leaving its fledglings unattended in the nest, or as Thoreau put it: "The victim is finally transmitted to the hands of the executioner as completely bare and destitute of feathers, as the callow young who are piping anything but melody in the deserted nest." Similarly, in writing his "Natural History of Massachusetts," Thoreau described the local fur trade with a certain proprietary pride. One trapper, he said, "takes from one hundred and fifty to two hundred muskrats in a year, and even thirty-six have been shot by one man in a day." A decade later, in 1853, he made a similar statistical entry in his journal. "In Brooks's barn I saw twenty-two gray squirrel skins freshly tacked up. He said that as many as one hundred and fifty had been killed this fall within a mile of his barn. . . . His brother killed sixteen in one day a month ago." Thoreau could object strongly to such killing, but the two opposed selves were never permitted to confront one another. He kept his mind protectively compartmentalized, for in the next year (May 28, 1854) he asked himself: "Do we live *inhumanely,* toward man or beast, in thought or act? To be serene and successful we must be at one with the universe. The least conscious and heedless injury inflicted on any creature is to its extent a suicide. What peace—or life—can a murderer have?"

Remorse About Killing

Thoreau [had] moments of compunction about killing, even if it was for study. Having just dispatched a box tortoise, he was temporarily racked with a fit of guilt. "I cannot excuse myself for this murder, and see that such actions are inconsistent with the poetic perception, however they may serve science, and will affect the quality of my observations. I pray that I may walk more innocently and serenely through nature." But even this expression of piety could not still the incident. It continued to agitate him. "No reasoning whatever reconciles me to this act. It affects my day injuriously. I have lost some self-respect. I have murderer's experience in a degree." One might suppose that such an extreme reaction would have a lasting effect. But less than a year later, June 2, 1855, a moth emerged from a cocoon that Thoreau had brought home and pinned to his window sash. He described its unfolding in the most admiring terms: "It was wonderful how it waxed and grew, revealing some new beauty every fifteen minutes. . . . It looked like a young emperor just donning the most splendid ermine robes that ever emperor wore." This extravagant appreciation concluded: "at dusk, when apparently it was waving its wings preparatory to its evening flight I gave it ether and so saved it in a perfect state." The man had no memory. Two years later, he commented, "I have the same objection to killing a snake that I have to the killing of any other animal."

In 1861, on his last trip to Minnesota with the enthusiastic seventeen-year-old naturalist Horace Mann, Thoreau, perhaps from the weakness caused by his developing tuberculosis, perhaps from a subsiding of tender scruples, put up with a plenitude of scientific killing, apparently without protest. Mann, for example, wrote his mother: "I shot two birds, Rosebreasted Grosbeaks, of which I had shot three before, two chipmunks and a gopher, and I would have shot a cart load more if my arm had not been so sore from the old gun kicking." Mann sent his kill back to Concord in a five-gallon keg of alcohol.

In "Higher Laws," Thoreau tells us that he long ago gave up hunting and even now feels twinges of doubt about fishing. But you will not find him telling you explicitly why either act might constitute unacceptable activity. He does observe that "no humane being, past the thoughtless age of boyhood, will wantonly murder any creature. . . . The hare in its extremity cries like a child." A good deal depends on how "wantonly" is defined. It does not seem that the intrinsic act of killing troubled Thoreau much. He tells us, "I did not pity the fishes nor the worms." Rather, he believed that there were activities to pursue that were superior. Thoreau flirted with Christian analogies. "Mothers should at last try to make their sons hunters as well as fishers of men," but what that cleverness might have meant to him is impossible to determine.

Dietary Concerns

What really bothered Thoreau was a subject that he abruptly broached in the middle of a paragraph. "Beside, there is something essentially unclean about this diet and all flesh." The statement is revealing, especially in the extension "and all flesh," for such ascetic revulsion was generally consistent with Thoreau's character. He continued in the same vein: "The practical objection to animal food in my case was its uncleanness." And he went on to speak with disgust of "animal food," of "flesh and fat," as grossness and filth, profoundly offensive to his imagination. At one point, eating itself seemed repugnant to him. "The indecent haste and grossness with which our food is swallowed have cast a disgrace on the very act of eating itself."

Occasional signs of tenderness did appear in the midst of this fastidiousness, as when Thoreau remarked that man lives largely by preying on animals, "but this is a miserable way,—as any one who will go to snaring rabbits, or slaughtering lambs, may learn." The choice of examples is interesting, since rabbits and lambs are particularly attractive and defenseless creatures whose killing any but the most callous might acknowledge was a disagreeable task. Thoreau therefore spoke on behalf of a diet of "a little bread or a few potatoes" and speculated that it was man's destiny to give up eating animals.

His sense of abnegation [self-denial] was radical, he realized: "If one listens to the faintest but constant suggestions of his genius [to the original formulation, Thoreau here added the next, intensifying phrase] which are certainly true, he sees not to what extremes, or even insanity, it may lead him; and yet that way, as he grows more resolute and faithful, his road lies." That is as fine and bold an assertion of independence as Thoreau ever made. At a moment such as this, Thoreau truly made himself vulnerable to the cynics of Concord, who were already contemptuous of the dietary faddists and other idealists who had invaded their community. But Thoreau was right to feel that he was, here, following his genius, for such scrupulosity in eating was everywhere evident in his writing, and Thoreau did well to recognize it. As he reflected on his position, though, he recognized the evanescence and doubtfulness of such perceptions. "The greatest gains and values are farthest from being appreciated. We easily come to doubt if they exist. We soon forget them. They are the highest reality." This psychological observation may explain Thoreau's lamentation over the crime of killing a tortoise for science, followed a year later by his emotionless anesthetizing of a moth. In any case, he realized that the logic of his argument might lead to an extreme that would be definable as "insanity."

To temper the vulnerability of his idealism, Thoreau interjected: "Yet, for my part, I was never unusually squeamish; I could sometimes eat a fried rat with a good relish, if it were necessary." Perhaps, although one always feels such moments partake of imaginative bravado. Thoreau was certainly more ironic here than the young man who wrote [sister of Emerson's wife] Mrs. Brown: "I grow savager and savager every day, as if fed on raw meat." But he still possessed an ascetic nature. No coffee, no tea, no wine. Only water.

Revulsion and Assertion in "Higher Laws"

That ascetic inclination joined with the increased coarseness and indifference that Thoreau discovered with some regret in himself. In 1851 he had observed in his journal: "We are more careless about our diet and our chastity." "But," he concluded, "we should be fastidious to the extreme of sanity"—an injunction that finally found a place in "Life Without Principle." Again, there was the note suggesting that fidelity to one's instincts could lead to madness.

This alternation between revulsion with animal life and an assertion of a personal coarseness capable of enjoying such dietary infamies as fried rat and raw woodchuck was visible throughout the chapter "Higher Laws," although, toward the end, Thoreau moved to a crescendo of confused abnegation. The problem for him was animal life. One was defiled by consuming animal flesh, one was defiled by behaving animalistically. "Gross," "gross," Thoreau chanted, "sensual," "sensual," "worms ... possess us," "worms ... occupy our bodies." Revoked by this "reptile and sensual" life, he emphasized its lowness by opposing it to the universal music of the "zephyr." "The wonder is how they, how you and I, can live this slimy beastly life, eating and drinking." Thoreau was obviously anxious to overcome that side of animal life in him that was fundamentally slimy.

Thoreau's Notion of Simplicity Can Help Save the Environment

Bill McKibben

Bill McKibben is a leading environmentalist and author who often writes about global warming and alternative energy. His books include The End of Nature *and* Fight Global Warming Now: The Handbook for Taking Action in Your Community. *Many of his articles have been collected into* The Bill McKibben Reader: Pieces from an Active Life.

At the outset of the following viewpoint, McKibben acknowledges that the Thoreau who assured his readers that "the sky is safe" could not have anticipated today's environmental issues and is of little help when it comes to technical matters. Nevertheless, he maintains, Thoreau can help us address our biggest environmental problems, which McKibben believes are rooted in our materialistic desires. It was Thoreau who framed the question "How much is enough?" and urged his readers to simplify their lives—to disconnect from society's demand to continually seek materialistic rewards instead of spiritual ones.

Understanding [*Walden*] is a hopeless task. Its writing resembles nothing so much as Scripture; ideas are condensed to epigrams, four or five to a paragraph. Its magic density yields dozens of different readings—psychological, spiritual, literary, political, cultural. To my mind, though, at the close of the twentieth century, it is most crucial to read *Walden* as a practical environmentalist's volume, and to search for Thoreau's heirs among those trying to change our relation

Bill McKibben, introduction to *Walden*, by Henry David Thoreau. Boston: Beacon Press, 1997. Introduction and annotations copyright © 1997 by Bill McKibben. All rights reserved. Reprinted by permission of Beacon Press, Boston.

to the planet. We need to understand that when Thoreau sat in the dooryard of his cabin "from sunrise till noon, rapt in a revery, amidst the pines and hickories and sumachs, in undisturbed solitude and stillness, while the birds sang around or flitted noiseless through the house," he was offering counsel and example exactly suited for our perilous moment in time.

Thoreau Could Not Foresee Today's Environmental Problems

He had, of course, no idea that he was doing so. Although he wrote often about the natural world, Thoreau lived at the very onset of the industrial age, and so knew nothing about parts-per-million, or carcinogenesis, or chlorofluorocarbons. One reads him in vain for descriptions of smog. Mass extinction seems unthinkable—instead, he is gratified and reassured by the profligacy of the living world: "I love to see that Nature is so rife with life that myriads can afford to be sacrificed and suffered to prey on one another, that tender organizations can be so serenely squashed out of existence like pulp—tadpoles which herons gobble up, and tortoises and toads run over in the road." His world was not used up, suffering—he was in the sixth party of white people to climb Maine's Mt. Katahdin, on an expedition that took him through the heart of that then-mighty wilderness. And though he could perhaps foresee the ruination that greed might cause (the East would soon be logged so bare that "every man would have to grow whiskers to hide its nakedness"), he had no inkling that we could damage the ozone or change the very climate with our great consumer flatulence. "Thank God the sky is safe," he wrote.

Furthermore, even if Thoreau had realized the challenges facing the modern environment, there's no good reason to think he would have pitched in to help. Reformers, he writes, "are the greatest bores of all," and I doubt a few hundred fundraising appeals from the Audubon Society would have changed his estimation that he'd received but one or two letters "that were worth the postage." More crucially, he was aggressively uninterested in the prospect of community that sage environmentalists now hold out as our great chance for salvation. The prospect of, say, abiding more closely with his fellows so that they could pool resources, live more efficiently, take pleasure in rubbing shoulders would not have appealed to a man who thought "the old have no very important advice to give to the young," who considered that two people ought not to travel together, who found it "wholesome to be alone the greater part of the time." Were Thoreau a modern third-grader, his report card would doubtless note his lack of social skills; it is no accident that he never married, and to imagine him with a child is a joke. There is a great deal he can't teach us.

You could even lay at his door, I think, some particular environmental problems. In his day, much to his disgust, people clustered together in Concord town and ventured out to Walden to cut ice; partly under his intoxicating influence, many many more of us have come to make our homes on the lake and ocean shores, in the scenic spots, far from the places where we work. There's hardly an unprotected shoreline in the lower forty-eight not lined with cottages and cabins; wilderness is now a selling point for the enterprising realtor. Even the suburb owes something to him; though clearly a corruption of his vision, in its splendid isolation the subdivision colonial retains a bit of his rude cabin.

Thoreau Cannot Help Us with Technical Problems

So to call him an environmental prophet—in many ways *the* environmental prophet, a writer of the highest value to the end of the twentieth century and the beginning of the twenty-first—requires that we think more deeply about what it might mean to live an environmentally sane life. It means recognizing the precise nature of the problems that we face. If those

Bill McKibben, author of this viewpoint, stands in front of solar panels as he talks to students in Montpelier, Vermont, about environmental awareness. AP Images.

questions are technical, then he is of no help. If our largest environmental problems are the result of something going *wrong*, some pollutant spewing unchecked from smokestack or exhaust pipe, then he's simply an interesting historical curiosity. Confronted with a smoggy city, I'd choose a catalytic converter over a pocket copy of *Walden*. And indeed we've nearly solved smog no thanks to Henry David. New equipment scrubs carbon monoxide from the exhaust stream of your car, which is why Los Angeles is cleaner now than a generation ago. New filters on factory pipes clean up rivers and lakes—that's why fish again swim in Lake Erie.

But what if those are not the largest environmental problems we face? What if we're really in trouble because things are going *right*, just at much too high a level? Consider the tailpipe of the car once more. It's not just carbon monoxide that comes spewing out, it's also carbon dioxide, carbon with two oxygen atoms. And this time there's no filter you can stick on the car to cut that CO_2; it's the inevitable byproduct any time you burn fossil fuels. It also turns out that carbon dioxide represents an even greater threat than smog: its molecular structure traps heat near the planet, triggering the greenhouse effect. The sky's not safe after all; the sky is heating up. And the answer has defied the technologists. They've managed to double the fuel efficiency of our cars in the last twenty-five years, but we've doubled the number of cars, and the miles they drive, spewing out ever larger clouds of CO_2. Scientists tell us they can see the extra heat, watch it melt glaciers and raise sea levels. To prevent it getting worse won't require some technical change; it will require doing with less, living more lightly. Our other biggest problems—overpopulation, habitat destruction, and so on—present the same challenge: they're inevitable if we keep living the way we do, thinking our same thoughts.

How Much Is Enough?

And it is here that Thoreau comes to the rescue. He posed the two intensely practical questions that must come to dominate this age if we're to make those changes: How much is enough? and How do I know what I want? For him, I repeat, those were not environmental questions; they were not even practical questions, exactly. If you could answer them you might improve your own life, but that was the extent of his concern. He could not guess about the greenhouse effect. Instead, he was the American avatar in a long line that stretches back at least to Buddha, the line that runs straight through Jesus and St. Francis and a hundred other cranks and gurus. Simplicity, calmness, quiet—these were the preconditions for a moral life, a true life, a philosophic life. "In proportion as he simplifies his life . . . he will live with the license of a higher order of beings." Thoreau believed in that same intense self-examination as any cross-legged wispy-bearded Nepalese ascetic.

Happily, though, he went about it in very American ways—he was Buddha with a receipt from the hardware store. And it is that prosaic streak that makes him indispensable now.

Thoreau Starts with the Essentials

In the advanced consumer society in which we live, How much is enough? is the first of Thoreau's questions that we must take up, the most deeply subversive question you can currently pose. We've been carefully trained to know that the answer is always: More. Once, researching a book, I taped everything that came across the world's largest cable TV system for a single day. I took my 2,400 hours of videotape home and spent a year watching it, bathed in the constant message that I needed so much. How much? Here's a commercial for Rubbermaid. "From the day I was born," a lady is saying, "I collected so much stuff." (The picture shows a sad family, hemmed in by their possessions.) "So we stowed our stuff in stuff from Rubbermaid." (Now the house is bare, save for big plastic boxes full of gear.) "Then we were so unstuffed—Hey! We need more stuff!" (Family charges happily out the door, waving hands in air.)

Thoreau begins at the beginning. He starts with Food, Shelter, Clothing, and Fuel. At the latitude of Concord, anyway, these have become "from long use ... so important to human life that few, if any, whether from savageness, or poverty, or philosophy ever attempt to do without." But of course each of these can be either simply or expensively obtained. He considers the possibility, for instance, of living in one of the tool crates that the railroads erect at regular intervals along the track. With a few auger holes bored for air, this did not seem "by any means a despicable alternative." As we know, however, he opts for something a little larger—the one-room cabin that he built from timbers recycled from the shanty of James Collins. He dug a cellar in two hours' time (Walter Harding, in his exhaustive edition of *Walden*, cites a study indicating that he moved 194.25 cubic feet of sand in this span, weighing 9.7 tons), then built a chimney, cut some shingles, bought secondhand windows, and eventually completed his home for twenty-eight dollars and twelve and a half cents.

This was a useful exercise. Building a house involves remembering that it's designed to fulfill a function—to shield you from the rain and snow, to enclose a volume of air that can be heated to keep you warm, to give you room for those possessions you actually need.

In Thoreau's case, that list included a table, which doubled as a desk, a chair, and a bed. It didn't include a closet, because the object of clothing is "first, to retain the vital heat, and secondly, in this state of society, to cover nakedness," and furthermore "every day our garments become more assimilated to ourselves, receiving the impress of the wearer's character, until we hesitate to lay them aside." In other words, he wore pretty much the same clothes all the time. There was no pantry to speak of; he subsisted largely on his beloved Indian meal, his rice and rye, his beans, his occasional visits to the homes of his friends, and a woodchuck which was eating his garden. In material terms, he was on a par with many of the poorest people around the world today. And he was like them in being a good, if unconscious, environmentalist. If you are worried about the largest problems, such as global warming, then to consume only a bit is the best remedy; according to one recent calculation, by Charles Hall of Syracuse University, a dollar or its equivalent spent anywhere around the world results on average in half a liter of petroleum being burned—to manufacture the item, and carry it to you, and advertise it, and dispose of it later. I was recently in a part of India where the average annual income was $300 a year—one-seventieth the American average, and with inflation taken into account probably about on a par with Thoreau's. Although I met not a single environmentalist there, each of those Indians had about one-seventieth the impact on the globe as each of us does.

Embracing Simplicity

The distinction between Thoreau and those folk, and it is a crucial distinction, is that he had chosen his deprivation—

embraced it, in fact, in the name of simplicity, philosophy, truth, so that it was not deprivation at all. And his heirs, I think, even more than the nature essayists who usually win the title, are that growing band of simplifiers whose books and seminars attract a small but significant portion of a population that has begun to feel materially satiated and desire something else. The best of these books is doubtless *Your Money or Your Life*, by Joe Dominguez and Vicki Robin, which has sold half a million copies even though the authors recommend checking it out of the library. They are unlike Thoreau in many ways; they seem to enjoy working with other people, for instance, and they write with a prosaic clarity that would make him wince. But their book owes much to his example. It is filled with careful accounting techniques, designed to bring home the same point that preoccupied Thoreau: "Money is something we trade our life energy for." Or, as the sage of Walden had put it, when a friend encouraged him to lay up some money for a trip to Fitchburg: "The distance is thirty miles; the fare ninety cents. That is almost a day's wages.... Well, now I start on foot and get there before night.... You will in the meantime have earned your fare, and arrive there sometime tomorrow." If the train stretched round the earth, he said, "I think that I should keep ahead of you; and as for seeing the country and getting experience of that kind, I should have to cut your acquaintance altogether."

Thoreau did not have contempt for money—it intrigued him, as his endless careful accounts suggest. But he realized instinctively the lesson that few of us ever learn, which is that there are two ways to get by in the world. The first is to increase income; the second is to reduce expenses. He went further than most of us will ever be willing to go, especially in his nonchalance about future security ("what danger is there if you don't think of any?"), but those that follow, like Dominguez and Robin, retain most of his radicalism, only in a more palatable form. And they play to an interested audience. Just as Thoreau reports constant visits from "doctors, lawyers, uneasy housekeepers who pried into my cupboard and bed when I was out," so the pollsters report that even to-day many of us remain attracted to some simpler alternative. When the Merck Family Fund sponsored a survey of attitudes on consumerism in 1995, 82 percent of Americans agreed that most of us buy and consume far more than we need, and 86 percent said our children were "too focused on buying and consuming things." Since shortly after World War II, the Gallup pollsters have inquired each year about whether or not Americans are satisfied with their lives. In 1955 the number who were very satisfied hit 35 percent. Despite the vast gains in material status in the subsequent four decades (only a tiny percentage of Americans owned a dishwasher in 1955; the microwave hadn't been invented), the number of people who identified themselves as "very satisfied" slipped to 29 percent by 1995. It's as if the twentieth century has served as a large-scale experiment to confirm Thoreau's hypothesis.

But if that is so—if the mass of us are at least dimly aware of our lives of quiet desperation—then why do we do so little to change?

Thoreau's Genius

To understand Thoreau's genius, remember that he raised this question in a time and place that would seem to us almost unbelievably silent. The communications revolution had barely begun. Advertising had not yet been invented, but the few shop signs in Concord, which we would preserve as quaint markers of a vanished age, appeared already to Thoreau as billboards "hung out on all sides to allure him; some to catch him by the appetite, as the tavern and victualling cellar; some by the fancy, as the dry goods store and the jeweller's; and others by the hair or the feet or the skirts, as the barber, the shoemaker, or the tailor." No Internet, no television, no radio, no telephone, no phonograph; and yet somehow he sensed all that this would mean to us. He did not need to see someone babbling into a cell phone as he walked down the street to sense that we'd gone too far; he was such a hypersensitive, such an alert antenna, that he was worried before Alexander Graham Bell was born. "We are in great haste to construct a magnetic telegraph from Maine to Texas," he writes. "But Maine and Texas, it may be, have nothing important to communicate."

It's not that he's in favor of ignorance or self-absorption. He was well read, politically committed enough to have engaged in Civil Disobedience, and obviously steeped in the minutest changes in the world around him (the precise quality of the ice, the texture of the mud). But he understood the danger of the big Hum—both the constant barrage of chatter from the world (two, three, four hours of television a *day*) and its lingering echoes. Even when you turn the set off, even when you hike deep into the Adirondack woods, your mind keeps up a constant vibration, playing and replaying words and images and ideas so that you hardly notice your surroundings. So that you rarely notice your thoughts.

Try disconnecting for a while and see what the hum has done to you, see what it's made of you. Thoreau liked his small library of books, but he recognized the danger even there: "while we are confined to books . . . we are in danger of forgetting the language which all things and events speak without metaphor." Often, he says, he laid aside his books and even his gardening. "There were times when I could not afford to sacrifice the bloom of the present moment to any work, whether of head or hands." He would merely sit in his door and the hours would somehow pass. Try this—see if you're still made for musing. How long can you watch a sunset before you get bored? How long can you look at the night sky before you seek some entertainment?

The idea that we know what we want is palpably false. We've been suckled since birth on an endless elaboration of consumer fantasies, so that it is nearly hopeless for us to figure out what is our and what is the enchanter's suggestion. And we keep that spell alive every time we turn on the radio or the television or the Net. Because when someone is whispering something in your ear, there's no way to think your own thoughts or feel your own responses. The signals that your heart sends you are constant, perhaps, but they're also low and rumbling and easily jammed by the noise and static of the civilization we've lately built. That's why Thoreau had to run away for a while, and it's why another small but growing number of people are beginning to question some of the premises of our Information Age. . . .

Only when we have some of that granite to stand on, that firm identity rooted in the reality of the world, only then can we distinguish between the things we're supposed to want and the things we actually do want—only then can we begin the process of satisfying "non-material needs in non-material ways," which environmentalist Donella Meadows has identified as our chief hope. Only then can we say "How much is enough?" and have some hope of really knowing.

Thoreau Aids Scientists in Understanding Global Warming

Michelle Nijhuis

Michelle Nijhuis is a science and environmental journalist who lives in western Colorado. Her work has appeared in National Geographic, Smithsonian, *the* New York Times, *and* Audubon *and has been featured on National Public Radio's* All Things Considered.

Nijhuis writes that both during his life and for some time after, Henry David Thoreau was seen as a shiftless squanderer of his own talents—even by his mentor and friend, Ralph Waldo Emerson. But Thoreau's fame has since extended worldwide, and, notes Nijhuis, his unique talents and lifestyle are being appreciated in new ways. Nijhuis explains that the observations Thoreau made and the journals he kept are now prized by scientists who can compare his careful botanical notes with their own in order to assess the ecological changes that have occurred over the last two centuries. In particular, scientists studying global warming can apply their findings to future environmental restoration projects.

The upright citizens of Concord, Massachusetts, didn't think much of young Henry David Thoreau. The cabin on Walden Pond, the night in jail for tax evasion, the constant scribbling in journals—it all seemed like a waste of a perfectly good Harvard education. Even more mysterious was his passion for flowers. "I soon found myself observing when plants first blossomed and leafed," Thoreau confided to his journal in 1856, "and I followed it up early and late, far and near, several years in succession, running to different sides of the town and into the neighboring towns, often between twenty and thirty miles in a day."

A Ne'er-Do-Well Makes Good

Thoreau planned to turn his vast botanical records into a book, but he died of tuberculosis in his mid-40s, the project undone. *Walden* and his handful of other published writings languished in near obscurity, and even his close friend and mentor, Ralph Waldo Emerson, said that Thoreau had squandered his talents on the woods. "I cannot help counting it a fault in him that he had no ambition. . . . Instead of engineering for all America, he was the captain of a huckleberry party," Emerson lamented in his eulogy of Thoreau.

Walden, of course, is now a classic of American literature, and Thoreau is considered a secular prophet. In Concord, tourists buy T-shirts printed with Thoreau's best-known sayings, including "beware of all enterprises that require new clothes." Much has changed in Concord. On the shore of Walden Pond in summer, warblers and blueberry bushes are still commonplace, but so are teenagers in shocking-pink bikinis.

Thoreau's unassuming gravestone, marked simply "HENRY," rests on a mossy ridge not far from the center of town and is decorated with pine boughs and pebbles left by admirers. On a sunny slope nearby, two botanists crouch in the grass, paying a different sort of tribute to Concord's famous son.

"We've got bluets. First time this year," Abe Miller-Rushing says.

"Are you sure you didn't see some yesterday?" teases his mentor, Richard Primack of Boston University. "First time," Miller-Rushing says with a grin.

The late April afternoon is clear and warm, and the slope at Sleepy Hollow Cemetery is dotted with the pale, four-petal blooms of the native plant. Were Thoreau here to marvel at the changes in Concord, these delicate flowers might surprise him most of all.

Thoreau's Botanical Observations

"How sweet is the perception of a new natural fact!" Thoreau remarked in his journal in 1852. Throughout the 1850s, while his neighbors toiled in their fields and offices, Thoreau spent hours each day walking Concord's woods and meadows, contemplating nature. His outings, he insisted, were anything but leisurely: "I have the habit of attention to such excess," he wrote, "that my senses get no rest—but suffer from a constant strain."

He taught himself to recognize hundreds of local plants, placing specimens in his well-worn straw hat. "When some whom I visited were evidently surprised at its dilapidated look, as I deposited it on their front entry table," he wrote, "I assured them it was not so much my hat as my botany-box."

The earliest blossoms and other signs of spring especially fascinated Thoreau. "I often visited a particular plant four or five miles distant, half a dozen times within a fortnight, that I might know exactly when it opened," he wrote. The author Louisa May Alcott, a Concord resident, remembered that the writer "used to come smiling up to his neighbors, to announce that the bluebirds had arrived, with as much interest in the fact as other men take in messages by the Atlantic cable."

Thoreau organized his eight years of botanical notes into detailed monthly charts, listing the first flowering dates for several hundred species. After his death, the dozens of pages of charts were scattered to libraries and collectors, forgotten by all but his most ardent students. Thoreau's data finally found a champion in Bradley Dean, an independent scholar, who supported his research on Thoreau with a trickle of fellowships and grants. Dean, who died in 2006, tracked down every page of Thoreau's charts, collecting a full set of copies at his home in rural New Hampshire.

Using Thoreau's Notes

Primack, 57, lean and sharp featured, had spent decades researching tropical forests in Malaysia, Central America and elsewhere before turning to his own backyard in 2002. Like Thoreau, he was interested in springtime, but his motivations went beyond a simple love for the season: Primack wanted to study how the natural world was responding to global warming. "Over the coming decades, we're likely to see a lot of significant changes caused by global warming—more and more extinctions, for example—but we can't measure most of those things yet," he says. "Bird migrations and flowering times are the best indicators we have that natural communities are starting to change."

Primack began searching for natural-history records from Massachusetts, talking to bird-watchers and amateur botanists. Through a former student, he learned that Thoreau, of all people, had collected exactly the sort of data he was looking for. In 2003, Primack called Dean to ask about his collection of Thoreau's charts. Dean, not at all surprised, said he'd expected that scientists would one day come looking for Thoreau's data.

Dean wasn't the first person to take an interest in Thoreau's record keeping. Sixteen years after Thoreau's death, an enigmatic Concord shopkeeper named Alfred Hosmer decided to continue Thoreau's botanical project. In 1878, and then consistently from 1888 until 1902, he recorded the first flowering dates of more than 700 species in the Concord area. A bachelor, Hosmer spent his Sundays exploring meadows, swamps and even the town dump. "Fred is . . . better informed about Thoreau's haunts than any man living or dead," wrote his friend Samuel Jones. "I, poor miserable I, *admire* Thoreau;

Fred *lives* him!" Like Thoreau, Hosmer turned his field notes into hand-lettered tables, sometimes pressing a leaf or flower between the pages. He died in 1903, leaving no explanation for his dedication.

Primack, joined by his doctoral student Miller-Rushing, now had detailed reports on Concord's flora from Thoreau and Hosmer, and it was time to compare the past with the present.

It's not easy to collaborate with dead botanists. Thoreau's penmanship was atrocious, and he used antiquated botanical names. Using the research of an amateur botanist and Thoreau admirer named Ray Angelo, Primack and Miller-Rushing deciphered Thoreau's and Hosmer's tables.

During their first year of fieldwork, in 2003, Primack and Miller-Rushing searched the sunniest, warmest corners of Concord, just as Thoreau had, looking for the first blooms. They found a place on the campus of the private Middlesex School where flowers turned up especially early. They talked a local farmer into allowing them to survey his fields. They walked the railroad tracks behind the site of Thoreau's cabin at Walden Pond.

When Primack found the season's first blue violet bloom on the gravel railroad bed, he was so absorbed that he failed to hear a construction truck approaching on the rails. The driver pulled up just 20 yards from the surprised researcher and angrily demanded that he explain himself. Primack quickly made clear he was no saboteur, but a botanist, and vowed to be more cautious. But as Thoreau himself surely would have, Primack and Miller-Rushing continued to inspect the tracks for flowers, paying for their persistence with a few run-ins with local police.

"We learned that if you're going to look at plants along the tracks, look at them briefly, always have a lookout and be ready to run into the woods," Miller-Rushing says.

In the spring of 2004, they began reprising Thoreau's work in earnest. With the help of several undergraduates, Primack and Miller-Rushing combed the warmest places in town. As they navigated crowds of tourists at Minute Man National Historical Park or stepped around the sunbathers at Walden Pond, they found they had a lot in common with their quirky collaborator. "We'd come out of the woods, sometimes covered with mud, and start asking people if they would move their towels so we could see the flowers," Miller-Rushing remembers. "That's when we realized that we weren't normal people."

Changes in Ecology

What they discovered wasn't quite normal, either. Primack and Miller-Rushing compared three years of their results with those of Thoreau and Hosmer, focusing on the 43 plant species with the most complete records. They learned that some common plants, such as the highbush blueberry and a species of sorrel, were flowering at least three weeks earlier than in Thoreau's time. On average, they found, spring flowers in Concord were blooming a full seven days earlier than in the 1850s—and their statistics clearly showed a close relationship between flowering times and rising winter and spring temperatures.

Primack and Miller-Rushing also found other naturalists who had carried on Thoreau's tradition of obsessive observation. Robert Stymeist, a retired accountant and devoted birder, frequents the trails of Mount Auburn Cemetery in Cambridge, a shady, arboretum-like spot that attracts colorful waves of migrating birds each spring. Stymeist, 59, has been watching and recording them for almost as long as he can remember: when he was just 10 years old, too young to be trusted with a key to the cemetery gates, he began sneaking into the grounds, binoculars and bird guide in hand. "It's just always been my spot," he says.

The ecologists' quest also led them to Kathleen Anderson, a great-grandmother and lifelong birder, who has lived on a wooded property south of Boston for nearly six decades. Born in rural Montana, she remembers that her mother rewarded her and her siblings for spotting the first bluebird or daffodil, inspiring a record-keeping habit that Anderson, now 84, continues to this day. Her elaborate daily diaries, shelved in her low-ceilinged farmhouse, detail not only family weddings, births and the news of the day but also natural phenomena ranging from bird arrivals to frog choruses to the newest blooms in her yard. "I guess I'm an old-fashioned naturalist—I'm curious about everything," she says. "But I never in my wildest dreams thought that these records would be of any significance. I even wondered if my children would be interested in them."

Like Thoreau's data, the records of these naturalists were idiosyncratic and tricky to analyze. Amateurs don't usually record exactly how long they searched for an animal, or how many people were looking, or how certain they were about what they saw—and these gaps make professional scientists nervous. "Scientists are used to analyzing other scientists' data," says Miller-Rushing. "We're not so comfortable venturing into the world of personal journals."

But Primack and Miller-Rushing found that the bird records from Mount Auburn, Anderson's diaries and data collected by trained researchers at the Manomet Center for Conservation Sciences on the Massachusetts coast all told a similar story. On average, migratory birds are turning up earlier every year in eastern Massachusetts. And as with the precocious blooms in Concord, the shifts in schedule are best explained by warming temperatures.

Global Warming's Disruptions

Even in the mythic American landscape of Concord, global warming is disrupting the natural world. Since Thoreau's time, average temperatures have risen more than four degrees Fahrenheit because of local urban development as well as global climatic warming. Concord, once a farming community, is now a busy suburb—Boston is just a half-hour drive from Walden Pond—and expanses of warmth-absorbing concrete and blacktop have created a "heat island" of higher temperatures in the greater metropolitan area.

Seasonal routines such as migration, blooming and breeding are the pulse of the planet, and everything from agriculture to allergy outbreaks depend on their timing—and, often, their precise coordination. "Pollinators have to be around when plants are flowering, seed dispersers have to be around when seeds are available, leaves have to be around for herbivores to eat them," says Miller-Rushing. "There are endless numbers of these relationships, and we don't have a lot of good information about what happens when their timing gets jumbled up."

While some flowers in Concord, like the bluets in Sleepy Hollow Cemetery, are blooming weeks earlier than in Thoreau's time, others haven't changed their schedules. Observations from Thoreau and other naturalists reveal that plants are reacting to temperature changes more dramatically than short-distance migratory birds, suggesting that climate change could divide plants from their pollinators. Spring's acceleration is far from orderly.

That's disturbing news, because many plants and animals are already declining in eastern Massachusetts for other reasons. Though Concord has more parkland and natural spaces than many communities, thanks to strong local support for land conservation, human habits have changed over the past century and a half, and habitats have changed with them. River meadows, once mown for hay, have declined, along with local agriculture, and many have gradually turned to swamp forest. As hunting dwindled, white-tailed deer began devouring woodland plants. Invasive plants such as Oriental bittersweet and black swallow wort have infiltrated Concord, even covering the banks of Walden Pond. "The woods are being re-populated by things Thoreau never even knew about," says Peter Alden, a Concord native and veteran naturalist.

Of the nearly 600 plant species for which Thoreau recorded flowering times during the 1850s, Primack and Miller-Rushing found only about 400, even with the help of expert local botanists. Among the missing is the arethusa orchid, which Thoreau described with admiration in 1854: "It is all color, a little hook of purple flame projecting from the meadow into the air. . . . A superb flower."

A National Network of Observers

Walking the well-traveled path that circles Walden Pond, searching for the earliest flowers of the highbush blueberry, Primack says his results make him uneasy. "I don't think scientists should just be studying things until they go extinct," he says. "I think they should be doing something to make sure they don't go extinct." He supports "assisted migration," deliberately moving rare plants and animals to new, more promising habitats. The idea is controversial among biologists, many of whom fear that the transplants could interfere with native inhabitants. But Primack argues that the risks are low and the need is pressing. "In the past, some of these species might have been able to move on their own, but now there are barriers—highways, cities, fences," he says. "We have an obligation to move them."

Primack and Miller-Rushing argue good-naturedly about whether certain plants and animals can adapt to climate change, but they, and other ecologists, know such issues are far from resolved. "Now that we know what's changing, what are we going to do about it, and what are species going to do on their own about it?" asks Miller-Rushing. "Those are unanswered questions."

For now, Primack and Miller-Rushing are helping other scientists build a national network of observers—ranging from schoolchildren to amateur naturalists to professional ecologists—to collect data on flowering times, bird migrations and other signs of the seasons. The goals are not only to understand how plants and animals are responding to climate change but also to fine-tune future environmental restoration efforts and even allergy forecasts. It's a project that will require Thoreauvian stubbornness.

"These things are almost always heroic efforts by individuals," says Julio Betancourt, a hydrologist with the U.S. Geological Survey and a co-founder of the national observation network. "Thoreau, and those that came after him, made a decision to make these observations, and to make them routine. To continue that for decades takes a lot of commitment and stick-to-itiveness and vision."

Thoreau's Methodology Can Help Solve Current Environmental Problems

Daniel B. Botkin

Daniel B. Botkin has served as professor in the Department of Ecology, Evolution, and Marine Biology at the University of California, Santa Barbara. He has also been president of the Center for the Study of the Environment in Santa Barbara. His books include No Man's Garden: Thoreau and a New Vision for Civilization and Nature.

In a speech given to the Thoreau Society, Botkin maintains that Henry David Thoreau's systematic approach to environmental issues serves as a guide for tackling current natural dilemmas. Botkin claims that even in the current information age, scientists often do not measure important information, do not use the information that has been measured, and tend to use improper information to try to solve environmental problems. He cites Thoreau's use of quantitative information about Walden Pond to debunk myths about the pond's depth. Botkin then refers to a current environmental issue, the demise of salmon in the Pacific Northwest. He asserts that the use of scientific methodology similar to Thoreau's can provide modern researchers with valuable data and potential solutions.

It is generally said that the modern environmental movement started in the 1960s with Rachel Carson's *Silent Spring*, and most people seem to believe that a concern about nature and the relationships between people and nature is a recent phenomenon. But the questions that today's environmentalists

Daniel B. Botkin, "The Depth of Walden Pond: Thoreau as a Guide to Solving Twenty-First Century Environmental Problems," *The Concord Saunterer*, vol. 9, 2001, pp. 5–14. Reproduced by permission.

ask are the same, ancient questions people have always asked. As long as people have written they have asked three questions about people and nature. The first is: "What is the character of nature undisturbed by human beings?" which in modern parlance becomes "what's wilderness, and what's natural in our terms?" The second is: "What is the effect of human beings on nature?" Its modern equivalent is: "Are we messing up nature or are we helping it?" The third is, "What is the effect of nature on people?" This question we phrase pretty much the same way. The last question is deep in Thoreau's writing.

For a while, when modern environmentalism first got started, it had to announce itself, so its proponents were argumentative. Then environmentalism became main-stream, and for a while—in the late seventies and early eighties—our society appeared to be moving to a resolution between pro- and anti-environmentalists. Public opinion polls have shown over the last twenty years that approximately four-fifths of Americans consider themselves environmentalists.

But in the 1990s, an increasing divisiveness reasserted itself and continues to underlie environmental debates. On one side extreme environmentalists argue that modern civilization will destroy the Earth's life support system, causing an end to life and therefore to human beings, and therefore modern civilization must be abandoned. On the other side, anti-environmentalists argue that environmentalists are going to destroy civilization, and we must protect civilization from them.

In contrast, public opinion polls suggest that the public concerned about the fate of the environment is also concerned about the fate of people. Most of us want to maintain both human beings and nature, both civilization and nature. This point of view is consistent with Thoreau's. So the masses, not the special interest groups, agree more with Thoreau.

What is the way out of the dilemma between the political and ideological conflicts over environment and the desires of the people to have both humanity and its civilization and to maintain nature? I believe that the writings of Henry David Thoreau have useful answers.

Ironies of the Information Age

During the more than three decades that I have been an ecological scientist and involved with environmental issues, I have found several ironies of our modern technological and scientific information age. The first irony is that often we do not measure what we need to know. I have been involved in a lot of major environmental issues, from the conservation of bowhead and sperm whales to the possible effects of global warming on forests. In each case I find that there are key pieces of information missing that nobody has bothered to find out.

The second irony of the information age thing is that, if we do measure something useful, we usually don't bother to use it. This is true among scientists as well as among public agencies and non-profit interest groups. We just archive information and forget it.

The third irony is that, although we have the ability to gather many kinds of scientific information, we tend to solve environmental problems from ancient myths, plausibilities, false inferences, and ideologies. This means we often start with an answer that we wish were true and squeeze whatever scientific information we use into a mold that conforms to this wish. And we get very upset if people do not believe us.

Thoreau as a Seeker of Quantitative Information

Here Thoreau is a wonderful example to us. Thoreau buffs are familiar with his search for quantitative measurements, his careful analysis of information, and how his imagination was stimulated by what he learned. His experience that strikes me the strongest is his measurement of the depth of Walden Pond.

A headstone marks Henry David Thoreau's grave in a family plot in Concord, Massachusetts. Farrell Grehan/National Geographic/Getty Images.

"There have been many stories about the bottom, or rather no bottom, of this pond, which certainly had no foundation for themselves," Thoreau punned in *Walden*. "It is remarkable how long men will believe in the bottomlessness of a pond without taking the trouble to sound it." He went on to write that "Many have believed that Walden reached quite through to the other side of the globe." And so he became interested in the depth of the pond and set out to learn this physical, quantitative characteristic of one of his favorite places in nature.

As a person with an intrinsic naturalist's and observer's inclination, Thoreau took a simple and direct approach to determining the depth of the pond: he measured it. He had the skill to do this, because he often worked as a surveyor. "As I was desirous to recover the long lost bottom of Walden Pond," he wrote, "I surveyed it carefully, before the ice broke up early in '46 with compass and chain and sounding line. I fathomed it easily with a cod-line and a stone weighing about a pound and a half, and could tell accurately when the stone left the bottom, by having to pull so much harder before the water got underneath to help me." Thoreau made an important step from informal natural history to quantitative measurement. This is a key step in using science to obtain a new kind of understanding of nature.

Once he had made one measurement, his curiosity was aroused and he began to investigate the general shape of the pond's basin. He made more than one hundred measurements of the pond's depth. From these he made a map, using his skills as a surveyor, and located the deepest point in the pond: "The greatest depth was exactly one hundred and two feet; to which may be added the five feet which it has risen since [with the spring runoff into the pond], making one hundred and seven."

His curiosity further aroused, Thoreau began to consider generalizations arising from his quantitative measurements. "As I sounded through the ice I could determine the shape of the bottom with greater accuracy than is possible in surveying harbors which do not freeze over," he wrote.

Measurements led to surprises. "I was surprised at its general regularity," he wrote. "In the deepest part there are several acres more level than almost any field which is exposed to the sun, wind and plough. In one instance, on a line arbitrarily chosen, the depth did not vary more than one foot in thirty rods; and generally, near the middle, I could calculate the variation for each one hundred feet in any direction beforehand within three or four inches. Some are accustomed to speak of deep and dangerous holes even in quiet sandy ponds like this, but the effect of water under these circumstances is to level all inequalities."

Thoreau's investigation then went through a progression to ever more general theoretical constructs, leading to the development of a set of hypotheses about ponds and lakes in general. To do this, he had to find a means to aggregate his data so that Thoreau could see the result as a whole and think about that whole. For him, with his experience as a surveyor, this was the straightforward step of making a map. This required that his depth soundings be located geographically.

From the map he "observed a remarkable coincidence," he wrote, "the line of greatest length intersected the line of greatest breadth exactly at the point of greatest depth." Now Thoreau had expanded his inquiry beyond the initial question of the depth of the pond. Having done a series of measurements, he began to see the pond differently, as if its bottom were a field, and he became curious about the shape of that field. Measurements had touched his imagination.

In reflecting on possible generalizations about his observations, Thoreau considered a comment made by somebody whose opinion he respected. "A factory owner hearing what depth I had found," he wrote, "thought that it could not be true, for, judging from his acquaintance with dams, sand would not lie at so steep an angle." In this process Thoreau was not the mythical hermit avoiding human contact, but a person who considered the judgment of others when their experience and knowledge might seem valuable.

At this point he was beginning to move into an interesting thought process. A simple curiosity had led to a simple measurement, then to a series of those measurements, which had then led him to a consideration of whether the measurements could be correct and, if so, what they implied. Here, it implied that ponds could not simply always be shaped along the edges like dams of sand. "But the deepest ponds are not so deep in proportion to their area as most suppose," Thoreau continued, "and, if drained, would not leave very remarkable valleys. They are not like cups between the hills; for this one, which is so unusually deep for its area, appears in a vertical section through its centre not deeper than a shallow plate. Most ponds, emptied, would leave a meadow no more hollow than we frequently see."

Based on his series of quantitative measurements, Thoreau began to speculate about the shape of ponds in general. He began to develop a hypothesis: perhaps the greatest depth of all ponds would tend to occur at the intersection of the line of greatest width and the line of greatest length. To test this idea, quantitative measurements were necessary. His scientific measurements piqued new curiosity, led to new kinds of questions, while leading to a new understanding. The new understanding brought him, in a different way than before, closer to nature.

Thoreau's study of the pond brings out another important distinction, that between observations and inferences, which are ideas that are developed based on a set of observations. A casual observation that Walden Pond looks deep is one thing, an inference from a single glance that it must be deep everywhere is another—it is a false inference. Confusing observations with inferences and accepting untested inferences is the kind of sloppy thinking often described by the phrase "thinking makes it so," and is something that continues to pose problems for dealing with nature and the environment.

Applying Thoreau's Approach to Modern Environmental Issues

One would hope that this sound, fundamental scientific approach would be followed today. After all, it's been well known and well applied for several centuries. And one would hope it was applied to modern issues about nature—the very object to which Thoreau himself applied the method.

But sad to say, I have found over and over again that today's environmental issues often receive as much scientific analysis as the people who chose to sit by Walden Pond and guess at its depth. Perhaps the situation that stands out most for me has been my work trying to help conserve salmon.

I have been involved with issues concerning salmon in the Pacific northwest during the last ten years. This began in the early 1990s when I was asked to direct a major, million-dollar project for the state of Oregon to find out what were the relative effects of forestry practices on salmon. Forestry is one of the four most discussed salmon culprits—always blamed for the supposed demise of salmon. Forestry is blamed because when forests are cut down near streams, spawning and rearing grounds for salmon are damaged or destroyed.

The other culprits commonly blamed for salmon declines are fishermen for overfishing, marine mammals—especially sea lions and harbor seals—for eating too many salmon, and dams and other waterway engineering for destroying the migration routes of salmon.

The study I directed was funded by a special bill through the Oregon legislature, so one would expect that the legislature, or at least the staffers, would believe that the information existed on which the study could be based. We assumed this to be true also. We established an office in Portland, Oregon. When we got up there we began to seek basic information. There were twenty-three rivers we were asked to examine—all the rivers in Oregon south of—and excluding—the Columbia River. We asked ourselves: What do we need to know?

First of all, we needed to know the numbers of adult salmon that have returned to these twenty-three rivers, year after year, so we could establish whether there had been a decline, whether there were clear trends over time, and what kind of variation occurred from year to year. We needed quantitative information just like the information Thoreau sought about the depth of Walden Pond.

From counts of adult salmon swimming upstream, we could determine what had happened to them. This seemed necessary information in order to establish a link to forest practices and the condition of salmon within the watershed of each river. And so we tried to get data for counts of the salmon on these rivers. We worked with the Oregon Department of Fish and Game and soon discovered that they had reports for only some of the rivers, about seven, and they were unable to locate copies of all their reports. They lacked an adequate archival system even for their own publications.

We examined the reports that they could find. Each had tables listing the number of adult salmon for each species returning each year. But we noticed that either in the caption for the table or in the text there would always be a statement that the numbers were "estimated." We did not know what kind of estimation procedures were used and began to ask. Each time we called we got an incomplete, fuzzy answer. Finally, I called the person in charge of the salmon management for the state of Oregon and said, "Just tell us where you count the salmon; we'll go down and talk to the guys who do the counting and we'll find out what they mean by 'estimated.'" He said "Oh, count the salmon. We only count the salmon on two rivers out of the twenty three." So, as Thoreau would have realized, one kind of primary, quantitative information necessary for our analysis was available for less than ten percent of the rivers.

Another piece of information we needed was a map of the current forest conditions, so we asked the state of Oregon for such a map. But they said they did not have one. We persuaded them to fund the creation of a map from satellite imagery.

Then we asked if they had historic information about the past condition of forests, so we could compare past salmon abundances with past forest conditions. At first they said that no information of that kind existed. But after several years of the project, we learned that about 1915 the Oregon state forester spent a third of the forestry budget to make a map of the forest conditions. Once he produced this map and left the position as state forester, nobody cared about the map. It ended up stored in a men's room and was eventually thrown out. However, that night a watchman noticed the map in a dumpster, and he rescued it. It was the only historic map done by the state of Oregon, and the fact that it still existed was because a night watchman, not a scientist or agency administrator, thought it might be important.

Next we asked about detailed information about the history of logging within the watershed of each river. If you want to know what are the effects of logging, you have to know about a river, what happened to the fish in it, when it was logged, how it was logged, and how much of it was logged. But we were told that in Oregon logging permits were given out by a county, and that these permits contained no information about where within the county, how much land, or by what method, the forests were cut. And the county throws out permit information after five years.

We decided to make a table containing basic information about each river, including the river's name, its length, the area of its watershed. We assumed this information would be easy to find. My research assistant called the Oregon Department of Fish and Game and was told that that agency did not have this information, and we should call the Oregon Department of Water. We did that, and we were told that that agency also did not have the information. The state of Oregon did not know the length of its rivers.

Without going into any further details, it should be clear that little of the necessary quantitative information was available. Then we ran into the second irony of the information age: even the information that exists is rarely used. None of the professionals involved with salmon, to our knowledge, had bothered to use the information about the counts of salmon on the Rogue and the Umpqua, the two rivers where the adult salmon were counted.

Thoreau, Experts, and Expertise

But then we found a remarkable exception. During our project we held ten public meetings. At one, Jim Welter, a retired fisherman in his eighties, spoke. He said "I don't know much about science, but it just makes sense that if these fish are spawned and reared in fresh waters and then go to sea for three years or so, that the number of adult salmon returning ought to be affected by the amount of water flowing three years earlier, when they were born." Jim, like Thoreau, went beyond an informal (what philosophers call a qualitative) statement. He went to the quantitative data. He obtained the counts of the salmon for the Rogue and Umpqua Rivers from the state of Oregon's Department of Fish and Game. Then he went to the U.S. Geological Survey and obtained records of water flow for those rivers. With help from a friend, he graphed these data. Once again he was taking the same steps that Thoreau did with Walden Pond.

Jim showed the graphs at the public meeting. They were impressive. A series of high water flow years were followed three years later by high numbers of returning adult salmon, while low water flow years were followed three years later by small numbers of returning adults.

There is another connection here to Thoreau. Those of you who are well read in his writings know that he respected foresters, fishermen, Indian guides—people who had direct experience and contact with nature, and he sought out their ideas. "Fishermen, hunters, woodchoppers, and others, spending their lives in the fields and woods, in a peculiar sense a part of Nature themselves, are often in a more favorable mood for observing her than philosophers or poets, who approach her with expectation," he wrote.

Jim Welter did not look like a typical TV news anchorman or TV expert. He was thin, wiry, wore a patch over one eye. But he knew what he was talking about and he thought clearly. . . .

The steps [environmentalists must take] are clear: first, learn for yourself if at all possible; second, if not, select your experts carefully—make sure they have had direct experience; third, listen to what they say and treat that as a hypothesis; fourth, test the hypothesis for yourself.

This is the path to knowledge we followed with Jim Welter. We viewed his graphs of salmon and water flow, and then made extensive statistical analyses to see if what looked to be the case held up under analysis. It did.

This way of selecting experts and using their knowledge was useful in our situation and can be useful today. It is not the role of scientists, as experts, to make policy, but to advise us about what is possible based on their knowledge and about how we can achieve the choices of the possible, what we gain and what we give up. Then in a democratic society it is up to us to decide which of the possible choices we wish to pursue.

Encompassing all these specific ways that Thoreau's life and writings can be of direct use to us in solving our environmental problems is his love of nature and his life-long search for ways to combine both a physical scientific and a spiritual contact with nature. These, and his love of learning and of civilization, are guides to us for today and the future as we struggle to find how we can conserve our surroundings and maintain the best that human civilization can offer.

Social Issues
in Literature

CHAPTER 3

Contemporary
Perspectives on
the Environment

Modern Thoreaus Share His Knack for Self-Promotion

Michael Agger

Michael Agger is a senior editor for the online magazine Slate. *He has written for the* New York Times *and* The New Yorker *and often reviews books and films.*

Agger writes that Henry David Thoreau's sojourn at Walden Pond was as much an ambitious attempt to make a name for himself as it was an experiment in frugal living. Contemporary followers of the famous writer have been even more shameless in their attempts at self-promotion. Fueled by environmental awareness, numerous authors have devised experiments in self-denial—and book promotion. Colin Beaven attempts to live in twenty-first-century New York City with no net impact on the environment. Judith Levine writes about her year without shopping. Mary Carlomagno attempts to give up a series of modern conveniences, from her cell phone to elevators. According to Agger, these studies in self-improvement and environmental awareness may be well intentioned, but it is often the less dramatic, incremental steps that truly improve individuals and the world in which we live.

W hen Henry David Thoreau retreated to the woods, he famously told his readers that he wanted "to front only the essential facts of life." What he didn't say is that he also wanted to front the essential facts of his ambition. It was at Walden Pond where Thoreau, an original slacker, finally became a writer. He finished his account of a canoe ride with his brother, *A Week on the Concord and Merrimack Rivers*, and wrote the first draft of *Walden*, the book that made his name.

Michael Agger, "On Walden Books: Are the New Thoreauvians Masters of Self-Denial or Just Self-Promotion?" *Mother Jones Magazine*, vol. 33, November-December, 2008, pp. 85–7. Copyright © 2008 Foundation for National Progress. Reproduced by permission.

An Experiment and a Gimmick

After 150 years, *Walden* endures as a monument to frugality, solitude, and sophomore-year backpacking trips. Yet it's Thoreau's ulterior motive that has the most influence today. He was one of the first to use lifestyle experimentation as a means to becoming a published author. Going to live by the pond was a philosophical decision, but it was also something of a gimmick. And if you want to land a book deal, you gotta have a gimmick. Recently, with "green living" having grown into a thriving and profitable trend, the sons and daughters of Thoreau are thick on the ground. Not many retreat to the woods anymore, but there are infinite ways to circumscribe your life: eat only at McDonald's, live biblically, live virtually, spend nothing. Is it still possible to "live deliberately"? What wisdom do we take away from our postmodern cabins?

The Modern Thoreaus

The most notorious neo-Thoreauvian might be Colin Beavan, a 45-year-old New Yorker better known as No Impact Man, and even better known as The Man Who Doesn't Let His Wife Use Toilet Paper. That last detail was the highlight of a 2007 *New York Times* profile of Beavan, which portrayed how he, his wife, and their two-year-old daughter were attempting to live in downtown Manhattan with zero "net impact" on the environment. This goal involves eating only organic food grown within a 250-mile radius, composting inside their small apartment, forgoing paper, carbon-based transportation, dishwashers, TV, and adhering to whatever new austerities Beavan dreams up.

Naturally, Beavan is hoping his no impact experiment has maximum impact. Like Thoreau, who, after all, was living on Emerson's land, Beavan is well connected. He has a book contract. His wife's friend has made him the subject of her documentary film, and he has a website, where people praise his boldness and question his motives. One commenter, Naysayer, speaks for the cynical: "Well, you've found your ticket to fame and fortune. Just undergo a period of time where you are inconvenienced (but plenty of exceptions) then cash in with book and movie deals, then speaking engagements around the globe." And then there are those whom Beavan has simply annoyed: "For the next year, I will be your polor [sic] opposite," writes Full Impact Woman. Unlike his deadly earnest spiritual mentor, though, Beavan views his project with an ironic distance, telling the *Times*, "Like all writers, I'm a megalomaniac. I'm just trying to put that energy to good use."

Beavan can be overbearing, but every ascetic choice implies a critique of those who aren't following the same path: I am giving up my car, therefore you are a selfish, earth-destroying auto addict. Also, extreme conservation—not flushing the toilet, not showering, and the like—can turn people off to conserving at all. Thoreau took it on the chin from Robert Louis Stevenson, who wrote of him, "So many negative superiorities begin to smack a little of the prig." The critique of Beavan is the same. These men have walled themselves off in a little hothouse of their own ego. They are not living courageously and independently in the real world, nor could they if they tried. Fair points, but what's the alternative? Every decision to try to live differently starts with a little showmanship.

Masters of Self-Denial and Self-Promotion

So the self-deprivation author must tread lightly: Bear witness to my extreme example, but realize that I'm just like you. Judith Levine, who charts her Year Without Shopping in *Not Buying It*, manages this balance gracefully. She goes on a spree before the pledge begins, and keeps in touch with her imperfection throughout. Yes, there is the thrifty virtue in resisting the latest, expensive fashions, but not buying also means becoming a cultural recluse. "An informed person like me needs to see new art, new films," Levine writes, longing for all the movies passing her by. She and her partner Paul discover that to subsist on free entertainment is to read dusty library books and endure bad performance art. Levine does experience the joyful liberation from stuff, and she temporarily gets off the hedonic treadmill. Yet she also admits that to not consume anything is to become a burden to friends, to feel old, and to develop an unholy craving for Q-tips.

Inspiration for these books can arrive in ridiculous ways. Mary Carlomagno, the author of *Give It Up!: My Year of Learning to Live Better with Less*, launched her self-denying quest this way: "While reaching for my black sling backs, an avalanche of designer shoeboxes hit me squarely on the head." Gotcha. She spends a month each giving up different things: alcohol, elevators, newspapers, multitasking, cursing, cell phones, and coffee. (Coffee is a common enemy in these books, including *Walden*.) Carlomagno is a less rigorous self-denier than most—the height of her deprivation is to give up dining out for a month. Yet she arrives at the same destination as do her peers: reading more poetry, taking longer walks.

While most of these authors accessorize their quests with some larger purpose, Sara Bongiorni, the author of *A Year Without "Made in China": One Family's True Life Adventure in the Global Economy*, decides to boycott China simply to "see if it can be done." Her book is marred by a faint jingoistic tone and a deadening obviousness. Guess what? A lot of the stuff in your house comes from China! (But not Hungry Hungry Hippos, apparently.) Toward the end of her year, Bongiorni debates whether to extend her pledge, but concludes, "A Christmas without Chinese gifts under the tree looms like a date with the executioner." Never has an attempt at conscientious consumption so missed the point.

In all of these self-deprivation experiments, there comes a moment when self-denial becomes self-defeating. An Internet entrepreneur from San Diego named Dave Bruno has received a lot of back pats for his "100 Thing Challenge," a goal to limit his possessions to that magic number. It's a useful thought experiment, but do shoes count as one thing, or should each shoe count as a separate item? The point—how much crap do you really need?—can quickly get lost in the details. Ascetics often become distracted by the rules or take things too far. Consider the fervent subculture of people who try to live plastic-free lives. Another perfectly worthy goal, but then you stumble upon advice like this on the blog PlasticLess.com: "Get a Vasectomy: Children are the target market for pointless plastic stuff. Most temporary forms of birth control involve some plastic packaging." (Uh, okay.)

Back to Basics Is Better

I don't mean to throw cold water on earnest self-improvement. But maybe we should set about such tasks in a way that doesn't reek of personal branding. Thoreau, after all, left the cabin behind, which earned the respect of Robert Louis Stevenson: "When he had enough of that kind of life, he showed the same simplicity in giving it up as in beginning it. There are some who could have done one, but, vanity forbidding, not the other; and that is perhaps the story of hermits; but Thoreau made no fetish of his own example." While that doesn't mean not writing a book, it may mean not letting the rigor of your experiment get in the way of the lessons.

All of these writers have good advice for our economically perilous and environmentally precarious moment. Not many, however, were permanently changed by their yearlong experiments. The authors of *Plenty: One Man, One Woman, and a Raucous Year of Eating Locally* welcome lemons and beer back into their house. Judith Levine is thrilled to buy new socks and starts to consume again, albeit in a more deliberate way. The ultimate lesson of the new Thoreauvians seems to be that change is rarely drastic. We must strive for continuous, daily, incremental improvement toward whatever social, environmental, and economic goals we deem important. That path won't land you on [National Public Radio's] *Morning Edition*, but it might just get you to floss, recycle, grow your own food, sit in the dark, air-dry yourself, take daily walks, and read more poetry. Which puts us back where we started: Walden Pond, 1845.

A New Hippie Movement Has Some Families Returning to Nature

Reihan Salam

Reihan Salam, an associate editor at The Atlantic *magazine and a fellow at the New America Foundation, has worked for* The New Republic, *the Council on Foreign Relations, the* New York Times, *and NBC News.*

Writing for the conservative British magazine Spectator, *Salam comments upon those families who have abandoned their materialistic lives in the city in search of a simpler, more environmentally friendly, rural existence. These dabblers in experimental lifestyles remind Salam of the hippies of the 1960s, who were ultimately conquered by consumerism and gave up their rebellious ways and hippie clothing for a mainstream existence of cultural conformity and power suits. This neo-hippie, back-to-nature movement has its admirable qualities, but Salam hopes its followers will move away to their rustic communes and stop badgering others about environmentalism.*

In late May [2008], *New York* magazine noted a highly unusual advertisement that appeared on Craigslist. A young Brooklyn couple had decided to sell virtually everything they owned, from electronics to furniture to designer shoes, for $8,500. As it turns out, the couple was planning on taking their two young children and setting out for the open road. Two weeks earlier, the *New York Times* profiled several other couples who had made a similar choice—to surrender their accumulated possessions and, with toddlers in tow, to leave a dreary, consumption-driven urban existence behind for something nobler and more environmentally sound. One couple, the Harrises, have been chronicling their adventures on a website called 'Cage Free Family', a clever reference to the cage-free hens so dearly loved by the ecologically correct. Though Jeff Harris had achieved financial success as a computer network engineer, he and his wife felt very keenly that they needed to reconnect with the land. And so the Harrises intend to leave bustling Austin, Texas for the greener pastures, literally and figuratively, of Vermont.

Voluntary Simplicity and the Hippie Lifestyle

Now, it could be that these back-to-the-land bohemians are mere curiosities, puffed up by *New York* and the *Times* simultaneously to delight and guilt-trip their status-obsessed readership. No one knows how many Americans are embracing 'voluntary simplicity', whether by becoming 'freegans'—that is, people who dive into rubbish bins for food out of choice, not necessity—or by abandoning suburban ranch houses to live in communes or campers. But my hunch is that these cage-free families represent the coming of a new hippie moment.

The hippies are now remembered mostly as foul-smelling, tie-dye-clad libertines who, when not covered in a thick haze of marijuana smoke or indulging in 'free love', could be found protesting against the Vietnam war or some other supposed outrage perpetrated by 'AmeriKKKa'. At the same time, the hippies represented a very American rebellion against the cultural conformity and political stupor of the 1950s. As the prime beneficiaries of postwar prosperity, the hippies briefly became the first 'postmaterialist' generation. After all, it was, and is, easy to be postmaterialist when all your needs are cared for by doting parents. So began a series of occasionally bold, at times ingenious, and often imbecilic 'experiments in living', ranging from the proliferation of middle-American ashrams to anti-authoritarian homeschooling, a cause later embraced by socially conservative evangelicals. The downside of all this is by now very familiar. Licence led, inevitably, to licentiousness. The patriarchy the hippies so bitterly opposed had the advantage of providing children with reliable material support, something children of the Me Generation couldn't always count on.

Consumerism Cracks the Counterculture

And yet a great deal of good came out of this fertile moment. America's technological leadership is arguably rooted in the tinkering of young techno-bohemians like [Apple Computer founders] Steve Wozniak and Steve Jobs and software visionary [and activist] Richard Stallman, who fiddled with computers out of utopian enthusiasm. As the left-wing cultural critic Thomas Frank argued in *The Conquest of Cool*, Madison Avenue eventually cracked this countercultural code. The hippie quest for freedom was co-opted by the capitalists. Consider the advertisements that, during the age of cheap petrol, showed hulking SUVs breezily wending their way through exotic landscapes, this despite the fact that in real life these monstrosities would inch along congested roads from subdivision to office park to supermarket and back again in a hellish loop of suburban torment.

The hippies thus traded in their shapeless garb for power suits, eventually giving rise to the corporate-cultural elite we now know and loathe—a group that manages to combine the self-righteousness and self-regard of the hippies with the shallow consumerism that made the 1950s such a drag, man. Lately we've seen the evolution of environmentalism, the hippie cause par excellence, into a consumerist caricature. Earlier this month the Discovery Channel launched Planet Green, a new cable channel dedicated to the green lifestyles of the rich and the vacuous. Suffice to say, the channel's agenda isn't to encourage less consumption so much as more expensive green consumption. It is apposite [appropriate] that the Prius is the ultimate bandage of a green sensibility—manufacturing its nickel battery is extraordinarily carbon-intense, and buying an ancient Toyota is at least as good for the environment.

There are, however, countervailing trends. Etsy, a much-buzzed-about internet retailer based in bohemian Brooklyn, directly connects consumers to creators of handmade goods. The goal, for founder Rob Kalin, is to spark a revival in the handicraft sector, and over the long term to build a new, more ecologically sustainable global economy. Granted, this is all slightly ridiculous. You can't build a flourishing economy on knitwear, eccentric earrings, and homemade pashminas [cashmere scarves or shawls] alone. But Kalin has tapped into the power of what you might call the dropout economy—the millions of bright women and men who are turning away from soul-deadening office work, and who are also turning away from what the left-wing Cornell [University] economist Robert H. Frank has referred to as 'the positional arms race'. The Harrises and Kalin are, in this sense, opposite sides of the same coin.

An Admirable Goal

Indeed, one can't help but admire the Harrises, and other families who've chosen to 'downshift' their consumption, for putting their money where their mouth is. Whereas others on the liberal Left rue consumerism and inequality, they almost invariably expect the government to step in and solve the problem by, for example, hiking taxes on the rich. You'd think we were children who couldn't help but work longer hours or buy expensive new automobiles in lieu of darning socks and eating thin gruel. What if the real inequality problem isn't a technical problem? What if it really is a moral problem? Not moral as in 'envy is a corrosive thing, so get over it'. Moral as in no tax hike will prevent people from building overlarge houses or custom cabinets at the expense of spending time with family and friends. A culture that is plagued by materialist excess won't be cured by taxes. It can only be cured, if at all, through a revival of postmaterialist values—that is, a revival of hippie values. Assuming Barack Obama is elected and he doesn't achieve paradise on Earth by 2012, it is easy to imagine a new generation growing cynical about politics and, like the hippies, deciding to beat the system in their own idiosyncratic ways.

I'm by no means convinced that consumerism and inequality are the worst things in the world, or that we are hurtling towards environmental doom. But wouldn't it be nice if all those who believed these things to be true moved to bucolic communes where they'd busy themselves with handicrafts instead of tormenting the rest of us?

All Americans Should Respect and Protect the Environment

Newt Gingrich and Terry L. Maple

Newt Gingrich was speaker of the U.S. House of Representatives from 1995 to 1998. He is widely credited as being the chief architect of the Republican Contract with America that ushered in a Republican majority in Congress—the first time in forty years—in 1994. Terry Maple is president and CEO of the Palm Beach Zoo in Palm Beach, Florida, and was professor emeritus of conservation and behavior at the Georgia Institute of Technology.

Gingrich and Maple argue in this viewpoint that all caring Americans, of whatever party affiliation and political philosophy, must have respect for the natural world. People are taught at an early age to love nature, and theorists have suggested this bond with the natural world is hardwired into our system. Therefore, the authors state, our stewardship of the natural world is a given, and the United States must take steps to ensure environmental health. Approaching this problem with the energy and zeal of an entrepreneur will help to solve environmental problems, according to Gingrich and Maple. The authors conclude that the United States must take a global leadership role to promote sound environmental practices around the world.

Who among us lacks a fundamental respect for the earth? Without respect, we would not bother to recycle or care for our gardens or brake for the errant squirrel. Parents universally teach their children to respect the environment, encouraging them not to litter or waste energy. We want our schools to reveal the many interconnections and interdependencies between the environment and our personal experience. For most of us, respect for the environment is not some far-out concept; it is an embedded value of mainstream America. Among the college students we have taught in Georgia colleges and universities, we were gratified to find near-universal expressions of respect for the natural world. From kindergarten to college, it is easy to teach respect and concern for the environment.

Childhood Learning

In childhood, family visits to museums, zoos, aquariums, botanical gardens, national parks, monuments, and wilderness reserves inspired us. The palms, peccaries, porpoises, porcupines, pythons, and other oddities we encountered in these natural settings sparked our youthful imaginations. These venerable institutions and venues still harbor a huge potential to inspire and educate young people; yet, they have been underused and underappreciated as community centers for inspiring learning, shaping attitudes, and changing behavior. Because they so effectively inspire and teach, our museums, gardens, and zoos should receive our full support.

Family trips to a museum or a zoo are always enlightening and a lot of fun, but we are fortunate to be surrounded by unbridled nature in our own backyards. If we just bother to look, we can see a vast population of fascinating local plants and animals in and around our homes. Our neighborhoods may be regarded as "community preserves" that most of us help to manage wisely if not diligently. Helpful environmental groups such as the National Wildlife Federation provide useful information on how to assemble and manage our backyard habitats. We eagerly create them at home, and we build them on the playgrounds of our neighborhood schools. The nearness of nature is an unavoidable and wonderful fact of life. It is here that respect is nurtured on a daily basis.

Some of the fauna in our yards instantly evoke respect. Butterflies, for example, have a special capacity to enchant and inform. Callaway Gardens, a botanical oasis just outside Atlanta, is visited annually by hundreds of thousands of people who want to experience the charismatic nature of these frail, enigmatic creatures at the Cecil B. Day Butterfly Center. The blinking blanket of color in constant, silent movement eventually captures the imagination of even the grumpy few dragged along by more adventurous members of the family. Children can never get enough of the natural world. Butterflies have other virtues; scientists have discovered that butterflies are highly sensitive to changes in the environment. A healthy population of butterflies is a sign that all is well; a precipitous decline is a sign of danger ahead. Respect and awareness are easily cultivated within a butterfly center or garden. An early exposure to butterflies will surely influence future botanists and zoologists, but the collective impact of these charismatic insects on humanity at-large is a greater and more enduring legacy. We know firsthand the potency of charismatic wildlife.

Environmental Challenges

Americans born after World War II grew up in a land and time that encouraged a heritage of optimism about the future. Doomsday scenarios depicting looming environmental crises and disasters are starkly out of sync with such a state of mind. We argue that they should be. The important lesson of the past few decades of environmental awareness, is that the interests of wildlife and the environment are better served by optimism and hope. The environmental challenges are real, but our imagination and innate creativity give us confidence that humanity, against all odds, can and will prevail. The overwhelming complexity, elegance, and grandeur of nature powerfully motivate our concern and our resolve to protect these priceless assets.

Newt Gingrich, politician, and one of the authors of this viewpoint, speaks on the importance of respecting the environment. AP Images.

The esteemed ecologist Garrett Hardin, in his benchmark 1968 essay, "The Tragedy of the Commons," warned that the earth and its life-forms were in grave peril. He argued that unrestricted access to natural resources and short-term thinking leads inevitably to depletion of the earth's limited resources. Consumers of seafood know the personal price when the tragedy of the commons is played out in economic terms. When shrimp, redfish, crab, and abalone are overexploited, their price increases, and the commodity is no longer available in the marketplace. The near loss of the Atlantic cod supply in the twentieth century is a painful reminder of the consequences when we fail to monitor and protect our resources. In some settings, privatization, an alternative to the concept of "commons," might lead to more accountability by the owner of a limited resource. As Hardin argued forty years ago,

> Maritime nations still respond automatically to the shibboleth [a widely held belief] of the "freedom of the seas." Professing to believe in the "inexhaustible resources of the oceans," they bring species after species of fish and whales closer to extinction.

In Hardin's original essay, the oceans form a "commons"—a place open to use by all. The ocean, unlike land, is not a place where a family or company has a vested interest in future productivity. Hardin suggested (and has yet to be proved wrong on this particular point) that the advantages to the individual of overexploiting a commons are much less than the disadvantages to the individual. Yet, the disadvantages to society (eventual loss or diminution of the resource) are much greater than the advantages (a greater supply for a brief period).

A False Solution

Hardin's solution to the problems of environmental overexploitation, however, does not ring true. He suggested the option of "relinquishing the freedom to breed." In an otherwise philosophical essay, his solution strikes us as disturbing, impractical, and highly undesirable. Families without children, with a couple of children, or with any number of children can all be good stewards of the environment—and our premise applies to all families in every nation. Indeed, in some respects, the population problem is solving itself, with birth rates falling as nations develop healthy economies with stable, predictable futures.

Overpopulation is a problem we can handle most effectively by targeting foreign aid and encouragement for emerging democracies with a stable rule of law and growing economies. Poverty and population explosions are highly correlated. We have learned much in the past four decades about the relationship between increased wealth and decreased family size and about the many ways we can reduce our environmental impact. As the "green" economist John Baden has argued, as people become better educated and wealthier, they demand an environment of superior quality. "In general," Baden concluded, "richer is greener." This is the principle that links the economy with the environment.

An Economic Answer

Effective economic policy is both a profound humanitarian act and a major step toward a better environment. By helping to guide developing nations into a more prosperous economic future, we will circumvent sixty years of failed economic policies in the world's poorest countries, and we will likely avoid further environmental degradation in the process. Thirty years of research, stimulated by Hardin's thinking, reveals that tragedies of the commons are real but certainly not inevitable. As ecologist Elinor Ostrom and her colleagues asserted in a 1999 article in *Science,*

> building from the lessons of past successes will require forms
> of communication, information, and trust that are broad
> and deep beyond precedent, but not beyond possibility.

Harvard biologist E.O. Wilson, who described his concept of *biophilia* two decades ago, offered another optimistic perspective on our relationship with the environment. Wilson theorized that there is an innate bond between humanity and nature. According to Wilson, people have a deep, even subconscious, affiliation with the natural world. It is a basic feature of our human biology. Most of us can sense this subtle feeling: during a walk along a beach, at rest in the glow of a spectacular sunset, or in the presence of majestic wildlife. Not surprising, Wilson, trained in entomology [the study of insects], experiences that feeling when he is watching ants. The phenomenon of biophilia explains why it is relatively easy to evoke sympathy for the environment and why we are filled with guilt when we damage or denigrate it. We seem to be endowed by our Creator with interest in and a sense of obligation to care for the natural world.

If caring is a natural propensity of humankind, caring can also be induced by contact with powerful and compelling naturalistic stimuli. None but the most jaded among us can avoid the feeling of awe that is engendered by visions of the Serengeti Plains, the oases of Okavango, the vast seclusion of the Okefenokee Swamp, the massive and majestic North American glaciers, or the volcanic forest habitat that is home to the world's last remaining population of mountain gorillas.

A Core Belief in Environmentalism

Is there an American—whether right, left, or center—who denies that such places must be protected? We know that our fellow citizens have profound respect for these and the thousands of other iconic natural places on Earth, even if they haven't visited such places. Yet, as generous as we can be when earthquakes, hurricanes, and tsunamis strike in remote locations of the world, our response to the myriad threats to endangered animals and plants or the glorious habitats on which they depend is too often tepid. Do we exert the resolute leadership that demonstrates our respect for the natural world and the species that live in it? Regrettably, our behavior does not always reflect the strength of our beliefs.

Our inertia belies the fact that we fit the description of "mainstream environmentalists"—we don't wear any special political armor; rather, we share the core values of appreciation, respect, and active stewardship for the earth. This grand coalition of parents, neighbors, pastors, teachers, and students, virtually every kind of person, is surely the largest interest group in America, but we must be activated by events or by inspiration. In this way, we are a kind of "silent majority." Family and future oriented, the sage advice of Theodore Roosevelt still resonates with all of us:

> The nation behaves well if it treats the natural resources as assets, which it must turn over to the next generation increased, and not impaired, in value.

Six decades after Roosevelt correctly connected American prosperity with American environmentalism, we have witnessed a host of new problems and opportunities. Somewhere in our zeal to produce and achieve, we lost sight of Roosevelt's insight and perspective. What would this great leader confide at the dawn of this environmental century? Surely, he would counsel commitment, cohesion, and courage. In the tradition of his vigorous leadership, we must face up to our responsibilities, roll up our sleeves, and get to work. With time and effort, the silent mainstream may become a vocal majority and a force to be reckoned with in the environmental arena.

The Entrepreneurial Approach

We are a wealthy nation, and some have argued that our wealth has led us to a state of arrogance and disrespect for the earth. This argument does not ring true. Our high-powered economy is sufficiently sophisticated and flexible to permit coexistence with a healthy natural world. We willingly create parks, monuments, and refuges; pass laws against pollution and the extermination of species; and live lives that demonstrate our appreciation for the value of ecosystems. Americans have expressed their respect for the earth in poll after poll. We have actively chosen to both live in the modern world and to avoid the tragedy of the commons. But if we aspire to a position of global environmental leadership, we will need to quicken our response to environmental emergencies, consistent with the goal of delivering to our heirs a world "increased, and not impaired, in value." Our business acumen and entrepreneurial spirit must be used in service of achieving a "more perfect" stewardship of the earth.

If we approach the environment with the zeal and spirit of an entrepreneur, we can accomplish much more than just the application of some bureaucratic band-aid. A promising example of the new environmental approach is a unique training program in environmental entrepreneurship established at the Foundation for Research on Economics and the Environment [FREE] in Bozeman, Montana. The program is designed to "explore the creation of new institutions and innovative public policies that promote environmental progress." Commentary in [FREE's newsletter] is refreshingly relevant. Entrepreneurial approaches to the environment are being honed in the West. It will be a major breakthrough when such programs are adopted by traditional business schools.

Although the label was not so widely used in 1970, we can vividly recall scores of entrepreneurs who invigorated the topography of the first Earth Day. Vendors hawked various new Earth products and publications to a curious population of largely college students. The prescient *Whole Earth Catalog*, published in 1968, was a gold mine of useful information that also emphasized alternative forms of energy. Entrepreneurs are optimists by nature, and they are not easily intimidated. In government and in industry, entrepreneurs who bet on big ideas such as renewable energy will eventually prevail over prophets of doom that buffer the status quo. We expect an Earth Day metamorphosis in the next few years as more people enthusiastically sign up for a revitalized, entrepreneurial environmental movement. Economists ought to revisit the symbolic power and imagery of Earth Day.

Corporate America is also evolving as it adjusts business practices to embrace conservation. Many American banks, for example, have committed to the World Wildlife Fund's Equator Principles, limiting investment only to companies and projects committed to environmental protection. Wal-Mart now only sells fish it has bought from sources that practice sustainable harvesting methods, as certified by the Marine Stewardship Council. Increasingly, business leaders regard our forests and wetlands as ecological assets that must be protected to support human life, public positions that their mainstream customers applaud. . . .

American Environmental Leadership

Strengthening the bond of people with the earth is the cornerstone of conservation. Although our affinity toward the earth is probably hardwired, as E.O. Wilson has asserted, that affinity must be reinforced in our school systems and promoted in our national and local media. We must work at the task to be effective conservationists. . . .

[We must] . . . confront the forces and events that threaten the environment. Such threats should not be denied; they are real. Americans are prepared by their history to respond to threats to the environment. We are a nation of individuals who willingly resort to teamwork when we face adversity. Historically, our forefathers consistently met and defeated formidable obstacles to a young, democratic nation. The wagon train and barn raisings are examples of team-building experiences integral to America's history. Early in the twentieth century, our nation bounced back from a frenzy of deforestation, and we instituted reforms to save farming in the American heartland. We know how to work together to achieve a better future; however, to lead the world, given a universe of demanding environmental priorities, we will have to first put our own house in order.

Although our nation's international leadership has been expressed in countless ways, when it comes to the environment our leaders have been timid and restrained. Other nations and groups of nations have attempted to lead and beckoned America to follow. They offered the Kyoto Accords that were rejected by resolution in the U.S. Senate on a vote of 95–0. The Kyoto document is clearly flawed, and Kyoto remains unratified by the U.S. government. Something should be done to achieve sensible reductions in greenhouse gas emissions, but our government has not yet demonstrated the necessary leadership to create a workable alternative to Kyoto. Our country needs to get back to the table. If a better international approach is negotiated, all nations, including developing economic powerhouses such as China and India, must be included. Leadership, therefore, is the highest priority.

Environmentalists Must Rescue the Planet in the Aftermath of Destructive Policies

Matthew Rothschild

Matthew Rothschild is the editor of The Progressive, *a left-leaning magazine that advocates for peace, social justice, and environmentalism.* Rothschild has appeared on Nightline, C-SPAN, The O'Reilly Factor, *and National Public Radio, and his commentaries have run in numerous newspapers, among them the* Chicago Tribune, L.A. Times, *and* Miami Herald.

Rothschild argues in this viewpoint that for eight years the George W. Bush administration pursued polices that were at best neglectful and at worst harmful toward the environment. According to Rothschild, world meteorological events have already fulfilled some of scientists' dire warnings about the consequences of such policies. With a new administration in the White House, says Rothschild, a revived environmental movement must take action to stem the advancement of global warming.

George [W.] Bush has committed so many criminal and derelict acts it's hard to figure out which ones are the worst of all. There's the Iraq War. There's the illegal spying on Americans. There's torture. There's kidnapping (I refuse to call it "extraordinary rendition"). There's the corruption of the Justice Department not only in its hirings but in its prosecutions. There's the outing of [undercover CIA agent] Valerie Plame, and the coverup. There's [Hurricane] Katrina. And many more: Just glance at [Ohio congressman] Dennis

Kucinich's thirty-five articles of impeachment and you can get a sense of the magnitude of malfeasance.

But one issue may ultimately loom larger than all of these. And that's Bush's abysmal performance on global warming.

George Bush and Global Warming

From beginning to end, his aggressive anti-intellectualism, his rich-kid arrogance, and his corporate allegiance have brought us the most backward and destructive policies imaginable—all at a time when foresight, not foolishness, was called for.

Let's review the tape.

He first denied the existence of global warming, and the human and corporate contributions to it.

Then he pulled us out of Kyoto [a worldwide environmental agreement].

Then his political appointees censored the scientists and edited, like some crazed Lysenko [Soviet director of biology under Stalin], the real science out of the policy papers.

He did nothing for six years about raising auto emissions standards, and then only reluctantly agreed to a change in the law that will raise fuel efficiency to 35 miles per gallon—by the year 2020!

He paid only lip service to solar and wind and other clean energies.

He did the same for conservation, which [vice president Dick] Cheney derided as a mere lifestyle choice. Bush and Cheney have just assumed that high demand was a given—and to put the blame on China and India if anyone complained.

For fiscal 2009, Bush proposed a 27 percent cut for energy efficiency programs and renewables.

Then, [in the] spring [of 2008], when Democrats tried to get a bill on global warming finally through the Congress, the Bush Administration prevailed on Republican legislators to put the kibosh to it.

Repercussions of Global Warming

While Bush and Cheney fiddled, the planet's been burning.

In July, two huge chunks of ice broke off the Canadian Arctic shelf. Scientists are predicting that the Arctic Ocean will be totally ice free during the summer of 2013.

Unusually powerful hurricanes, like Katrina and Rita, have kicked up, just as scientists predicted.

So, too, did they predict the increasing number of tornadoes, the record heavy rains, the intense droughts, and the more frequent wildfires that we've been seeing.

It's likely to get worse.

If we don't take drastic action very soon, "hundreds of millions of people would become refugees" this century, NASA scientist [and climatologist] James Hansen testified to Congress on June 23[, 2008]. "Polar and alpine species will be pushed off the planet." Mountain glaciers will melt, lakes will dry up, and coral reefs will be destroyed, he predicted.

"We have already gone too far," said Hansen. "Time is running out."

So what does Bush do in his last visit to Europe at the G8 summit on global warming? He essentially gives the world the finger. After bollixing up any possibility of an agreement there, he took his final bow and said: "Goodbye from the world's biggest polluter."

What a guy!

Future Hopes

Fortunately, his successor is bound to be better. Barack Obama calls global warming "one of the greatest moral challenges of our generation." He has proposed reducing carbon emissions by 80 percent below 1990 levels by 2050. He wants to invest $150 billion in the next ten years in clean energy, and by 2025, he wants 25 percent of electricity consumed in the United States to be "derived from clean, sustainable energy sources, like solar, wind, and geothermal," his website says.

(He also is getting a lot of financial support from nuclear power companies, though his website is mum on nuclear.). . .

More needs to be done than . . . Obama . . . has proposed. Al Gore is once again showing the way on this issue. On July 17[, 2008], he issued a challenge to the nation to produce "100 percent of our electricity from renewable energy and truly carbon-free sources within ten years. This goal is achievable, affordable, and transformative," he said. "It represents a challenge to all Americans, in every walk of life: to our political leaders, entrepreneurs, innovators, engineers, and to every citizen."

Gore said that the price of solar, wind, and geothermal power is going down and becoming affordable, just as the price of oil and coal is going out of sight. This has "radically changed the economics of energy," he said.

The potential for getting off of carbon-based fuels is abundant.

"Enough solar energy falls on the surface of the Earth every forty minutes to meet 100 percent of the entire world's energy needs for a full year," Gore said.

"Tapping just a small portion of this solar energy could provide all of the electricity America uses. And enough wind power blows through the Midwest corridor every day to also meet 100 percent of U.S. electricity demand."

Senator Bernie Sanders of Vermont has proposed one of the most forward-looking pieces of legislation to bring us down the path that Gore is blazing.

On July 7[, 2008], he introduced a bill entitled the "10 Million Solar Roofs Act of 2008." It would require the Secretary of Energy to set up a program to provide rebates to individuals, businesses, and government buildings so they can put up solar panels on their roofs. Sanders's goal is to put up panels on ten million roofs in the next decade.

The rebate could account for up to "50 percent of the cost of the purchase and installation of the system," the bill says.

Environmental writer and adventurer Guy Grieve enjoys the banks of Walden Pond. Henry David Thoreau lived on Walden Pond from 1845 to 1847. © Rick Friedman/Corbis.

To qualify for the rebates, homeowners and businesses must demonstrate that they meet tough standards for energy efficiency.

In his bill, Sanders extols the promise of solar energy.

"There is a huge potential for increasing the quantity of electricity produced in the United States from distributed solar photovoltaics," it says. "The use of photovoltaics on the roofs of 10 percent of existing buildings could meet 70 percent of peak electric demand."

It would also be good for the economy.

"Investments in renewable energy stimulate the development of green jobs that provide substantial economic benefits," the bill states. Sanders is hopeful about this initiative. "We can reverse greenhouse gas emissions," he says. "We can break our dependence on foreign oil."

The Corporate Problem

But to pass Sanders's bill, much less to arrive at Gore's destination of a carbon-free grid, will require confronting corporate power. Gore himself pointed out the problem.

"The greatest obstacle to meeting the challenge of 100 percent renewable electricity in ten years may be the deep dysfunction of our politics and our self-governing system as it exists today," he said. "In recent years, our politics has tended toward incremental proposals made up of small policies designed to avoid offending special interests. . . . Our democracy has become sclerotic [unable or hesitant to adapt] at a time when these crises require boldness."

James Hansen was even blunter. Testifying exactly twenty years after he first alerted Congress to the looming problem of global warming, Hansen said the "changes needed to preserve Creation, the planet on which civilization developed, are clear. But the changes have been blocked by special interests, focused on short-term profits, who hold sway in Washington and other capitals."

Placing the blame squarely on the shoulders of the fossil fuel companies, Hansen said they chose to "spread doubt about global warming, as tobacco companies discredited the smoking-cancer link." He called the [2008] elections "critical for the planet," and he urged Americans to "turn out to pasture the most brontosaurian Congressmen."

But the problem that Hansen and Gore identify so well won't be solved simply by electing a few better members to Congress and a President who doesn't have his head in the sands of Saudi Arabia.

No, the problem won't be solved until we break the corporate stranglehold on our democracy. To do that, we need an organized, energized grassroots movement to use its power to overwhelm that of the ExxonMobils and the Halliburtons. And we need this movement to keep the pressure on Bush's successor so he doesn't backslide but moves forward toward the bold vision that Gore has offered.

Creating this movement may seem as difficult as transitioning off of oil and coal. But it need not be. There is a tremendous hunger, especially among young people, to take on the challenge of global warming. And there is a great urgency, among those of us in our later years, to attend to this problem before it's too late.

We all know who wields power in this country. It's the same group that has been polluting the Earth while it profits from fossil fuels.

We need to take its power away.

A reinvigorated green movement may end up not only saving the planet but saving our democracy, as well.

Environmentalism Is the New Religion of Urban Atheists

Kevin Steel

Kevin Steel has served on the staff of such publications as Western Standard *and* Alberta Report. *His work has appeared in the* National Post, The American Spectator, Alberta Views, *and* The Canadian Encyclopedia.

Writing for the conservative Canadian magazine Western Standard, *Steel notes the similarities between the environmental movement and organized religion. Two similarities in particular are the lost garden motif (vs. the biblical Garden of Eden) and the apocalyptic myth (vs. the biblical Revelation). When people lose their religion, Steel observes, they replace it not with nothing, but with anything. He says that environmentalism has filled that void for many contemporary urban nonbelievers. Whether it will grow into a full-fledged religion or not is arguable, but Steel wonders if the same leftists who uphold the separation of church and state will do so with regard to the new religion of environmentalism.*

If anyone has doubts that environmentalism has become a religion, then Al Gore, the failed U.S. presidential candidate who has been born again as a global warming guru, will put those doubts to rest. At the national convention of the American Institute of Architects in San Antonio on May 5[, 2007], Gore continually spoke of how global warming had prompted "a new way of thinking" to save the planet. "It's in part a spiritual crisis," Gore preached. "It's a crisis of our own self-definition—who we are. Are we creatures destined to destroy our own species? Clearly not." Gore's ideas don't just have religious overtones, they are religious: spirituality, apocalypse, destiny, conversion, salvation.

Environmental Prophets

That Gore would be talking "spiritual" about the environment, even to a crowd of yawning architects in Texas, is not surprising. His Oscar-winning documentary about global warming, *An Inconvenient Truth*, is itself something of a leap of faith, so poorly does it represent the science on climate. Flawed though the film was, it proved popular enough to catapult Gore onto the speaking circuit, where he now commands $125,000 an appearance to sermonize about the "spiritual crisis." He is environmentalism's most popular itinerant preacher.

Gore might blanch at the idea of being called a prophet because of the religious connotations, but, more and more, environmentalism has taken on the characteristics of a religion. In Canada, Green party Leader Elizabeth May has been merging environmentalism and religion. On April 29[, 2007], she delivered a guest sermon on climate change at the Wesley Knox United Church in London, Ont. Introduced to the congregation by a Liberal MP as a "prophet," May's over-the-top sermon made instant headlines. She took aim at fundamentalist Christians in the U.S.: "They are waiting for the end time in glee, and they unfortunately include President [George W.] Bush." She said that the Harper government's approach to climate change "represents a grievance worse than [British] Neville Chamberlain's appeasement of the Nazis." Her message couldn't have been clearer: they are evil; hers is the only road to salvation.

A Dangerous Trend

In the 1960s, a few environmentalists actually believed their cause could not succeed unless it became a religion first. How close they've come to attaining that goal in a generation is perhaps best gauged by the growing body of chroniclers and critics of the new religion.

In 2003, author Michael Crichton kick-started the criticism with a widely circulated speech to the Commonwealth Club in San Francisco. Crichton, who has written such best-selling novels as *State of Fear* and *Jurassic Park*, pinpointed the main practitioners. "Environmentalism seems to be the religion of choice for urban atheists," Crichton said, right after ranking it as "one of the most powerful religions in the western world." Crichton maintains the position that while an environmental movement is necessary, the conversion of the movement to religion is dangerous. His goal is to get the movement out of the "clutches of religion, and back to a scientific discipline."

Myron Ebell, director of energy and global warming policy at the Competitive Enterprise Institute in Washington, D.C., doesn't know if that's possible. "It's almost trite to say it because it's quoted so much, but G.K. Chesterton said, 'When people stop believing in God, they don't believe in nothing—they believe in anything.' The loss of connection to the practice of Christianity, and in some cases Judaism, has left a lot of people with utterly meaningless lives," Ebell says. As they discover that, they want to find something. Environmentalism—saving the planet—fills the void.

Environmental Theology

Modern society is seeing an invasion of environmental morality. The green cause now influences what kinds of cars we drive, or even whether we should drive, what kinds of houses we buy, what we wear, what we eat, what we do each day with our garbage, and even, for some, how many children they will have. A May 7[, 2007,] news story in the London *Sunday Times* paraphrased a new report from a green think-tank, Optimum Population Trust: "Having large families should be frowned upon as an environmental misdemeanor in the same way as frequent long-haul flights, driving a big car and failing to reuse plastic bags." Why? Because it turns out couples who had two children instead of three "could cut their family's carbon dioxide output by the equivalent of 620 return flights a year between London and New York."

If equating your children to the exhaust of a transatlantic jetliner doesn't strike you as particularly religious, you might not be seeing the bigger picture. In a Jan. 9 column in the *Financial Times*, British economist John Kay noted that environmentalism now provided "a simple, all-encompassing narrative," with two key myths that anthropologists point out are common to many cultures, though they appear to have developed independently: the myth of the Fall (or the Lost Eden), and an apocalypse myth.

The Fall in environmental theology is the idea that our modern, material lives have put us out of harmony with nature and that humanity needs to return to a "natural" state in order to achieve balance. It is a myth because mankind never lived in a static natural state, but has been constantly evolving and learning to use nature throughout time. Some environmentalists push this idea to the extreme and contend that the natural state of the world is one without mankind altogether.

The Apocalypse Myth

The apocalypse myth is the one that Al Gore has been preaching: global warming doom. Kay observes that for years, the environmental movement didn't have a successful apocalypse myth because in most cases, the environment has been getting healthier, due to greater public awareness and better technology. "The discovery of global warming filled a gap in the canon. That is why environmentalists attach so much importance to the assertion not just that the world is warming up, which is plainly true, but that this warming is our fault, which is less plainly true," Kay writes.

It is in the global warming apocalyptic myth that many environmentalists take their leap of faith. This makes sense because prophecy has typically been the preserve of religion since the days of the Delphic Oracle and before. David Orrell, a computational scientist and author of *Apollo's Arrow: The Science of Prediction and the Future of Everything*, says the science of climate change has definitely taken on some religious aspects. In particular, he sees what he calls a "priestly class" developing, a "class of people who are interested in protecting their own version of the world. That's the sense I get with some of these scientific models of the atmosphere," Orrell says. Most of the predictions from these models are so vague they are in fact quite useless, he contends, but nobody appears to be questioning them. "Scientists are famous for their skepticism, but when it comes to predictions, their skepticism seems to be put on hold."

Faith in Environmentalism

Not all who label environmentalism a religion view it harshly. Thomas Dunlap, a professor of history at Texas A&M University, in his book *Faith in Nature: Environmentalism as a Religious Quest*, treats it with a great deal of respect. Dunlap, a devout Catholic, writes, "Environmentalists do not, generally, believe the movement constitutes a religion (and in conventional terms it does not) and they are uncomfortable with religious terms, but they ask religious questions: what purpose do humans have in the universe, and what must they do to fulfil it?" Dunlap sees environmentalism as a nascent religion, one that has not fully worked out its moral imperatives but is worthy of the same kind of respect that other great religious impulses deserve.

William Cronon, professor of history and environmental studies at the University of Wisconsin, wrote the foreword to Dunlap's book and also defends the notion of environmentalism as religion. "If you take it as your premise that faith or belief in things in the world that cannot be proven is by definition proof of unreliability, then there are as many reasons to be doubtful of environmentalism as there are reasons to be doubtful of Christianity or Judaism or Islam or any other great religious tradition," Cronon says. There are many things in the world that matter enormously that we can never prove with one hundred per cent certainty. Human beings always act on partial knowledge, which means we always act in part on faith. "Science believes, and I agree with this, that we should test our assumptions about the world and subject them to criticism. My own belief is that any religious practice should also subject itself to that kind of scrutiny. I would say the great religious traditions do that," says Cronon.

How environmentalism as religion would fare when subjected to postmodern western political traditions is another thing altogether. Today, the separation of church and state is guarded jealously by secularists such as the American Civil Liberties Union. How such groups—and religions with differing views on the morality of having children—might respond to environmentalism as a new state religion is not yet known. It's an unpredictable world. As environmentalists might say: have faith.

It Is Not Too Late to Save the Environment

Zoe Cormier

Zoe Cormier is a journalist and science writer. She has written for The Ecologist, Plenty *magazine, and* The Toronto Star *and has served as a columnist, writing "The Green Report," on environmental research, news, and trends in London's* Globe and Mail.

As a science writer, Cormier came to environmentalism because so many of her assignments were about the subject. What she learned was not uplifting. The planet is in poorer shape than most people suspect, and it's getting worse. As Cormier investigated environmental topics, her findings literally made her cry: there were so many tragic tales of harmful waste ruining people's health. Cormier argues that there must be a sustained and worldwide effort to clean up the environment before a third of all species become extinct. Individuals can do their part at home by being more attuned to what they buy and use. On a global scale, there is still time to make a difference. With proper legislation and subsequent environmental efforts, Cormier believes we can prevent a worldwide catastrophe.

I never planned to be a specialist in environmental reporting. I started my career in journalism doing mostly straight science writing—articles that required the translation of scientific mumbo-jumbo into accessible language. Genetics, technology, medicine—the usual. But the bulk of my assignments quickly came to be on environmental issues. The media are devoting more space to them as the public wants to under-

Zoe Cormier, "A Way Without the Will: Bad Choices Lead to Bad Outcomes," *This Magazine*, vol. 42, September-October 2008, pp. 11–12. Copyright © 2008 Red Maple Foundation. Reproduced by permission.

stand and deal with the mess we've made. A science degree came in handy for translating the importance of neurotoxins and greenhouse gases.

Things Are Bad

But lately it's made me feel a bit like a [mythological prophet] Cassandra, cursed forever to preach grim environmental truths that no one wants to heed. Here it is: things are bad. probably much worse than you think, and the most maddening part is that I believe we *could* fix things—we just won't.

I'd always cared about the environment, but until it became a professional necessity, I didn't study it formally. When I was a student at the University of Toronto, I didn't want to spend every day feeling bummed out about how stupid and greedy people are and what a sullied planet I've inherited.

Instead, I wanted to study something that would make me happy. So I studied zoology. Learning about how living things work gives me constant wonder and joy. Most people don't think of it this way, but biology provides incredible fodder for the imagination. All you have to do is look at the spiral of your own inner ear, leopard slug sex (YouTube it, seriously), the architecture of spider silk, the development of frog embryos or the complexities of the genetic code to see that this is true. Humans might be able to put a man on the moon and memorize pi to thousands of decimal places, but we will never create something as complex as a bacterium—let alone ourselves. Every day I learned something new that blew my mind, and every day I had fun doing it.

I only started to really learn about environmental issues in earnest in the fourth year of my Bachelor of Science degree, when I took a course on climate change ecology. I was still learning something new and mind-blowing every day—but it wasn't fun anymore.

I thought I was well-informed. I knew that things were bad, but *this* bad? The world's great coral reefs might disappear by the time I'm 40? The highest concentrations of PCBs on earth are found in the breast milk of Inuit women? A third of all species might be destined for extinction (or already gone) by 2050?

These weren't the hyperbolic ravings of unshod hippies— this was top-calibre, peer-reviewed science taught at one of our country's top universities. This wasn't on the fringes of academia. This was the main fare.

Worse than Imagined

In my first year doing environmental journalism—and I am embarrassed to admit this—I cried constantly. Just a few months after starting out as a freelancer, I was sent by a magazine to visit Aamjiwnaang, a First Nations reserve in Ontario that is surrounded by chemical factories, after being convinced/conned by the Crown to sell their ancestral land to Shell, Dow, Sunoco and other petro-giants. Now, fringed by industrial smokestacks, the people there are plagued by a host of health problems, including rampant asthma, far-too-frequent miscarriages and what appears to be one of the most skewed birth ratios in the world (twice as many girls are born as boys—the oil industry contends it is little more than a coincidence).

Again, as a city-bred white girl with little reason to complain: I cried. A lot. Not just because of that one unfair, stupid mess, but for all the unfair stupid messes like it all over the world. The strange tingly headaches and difficulty breathing I suffered while I was visiting the region—neither of which I would consider psychosomatic—didn't help.

Now it is my job to know about every shred of environmental news and research that comes through the wires. And let me tell you: things are seriously messed up. Things are so much worse than you think they are.

It's not that I think the ice caps will melt tomorrow and we're all going to die horribly in some kind of apocalyptic

President Bill Clinton, musician Don Henley, and First Lady Hillary Rodham Clinton walk down a path in Walden Woods for the opening of the Thoreau Institute in 1998. Henley, former drummer of the 1970s band the Eagles, leads an organization dedicated to preserving Walden Pond. Paul J. Richards/AFP/Getty Images.

Day After Tomorrow affair. I don't think we are going to wipe out all life on earth and the planet will become uninhabitable—life is far more resilient than that.

What I do think is that the world is going to change a lot over the next century. And I think the changes are going to be very uncomfortable. Energy, food, water and everything else will be more expensive and scarce.

But most of all—and for me this is the most heartbreaking thing—I do believe that a staggering proportion of life on earth will go extinct. No one really knows how much, but probably a third of amphibians, a quarter of mammals, and probably more than a third of all species. Period. Our world will be less diverse, less colourful and a lot less interesting. To an animal geek like me, it means a much more dull and lonely world.

We Can Clean Up This Mess

But as bad as things are, I don't cry or freak out anymore—worrying all the time and losing sleep won't do any good, and I'll just ruin my own health. So I just do what I can to make the world a better place, and the rest of the time, carpe diem [seize the day] and carpe nocte [seize the night]: enjoy my own life while I can, before things get much worse (because they will).

But this is the sad irony: as pessimistic as I am, I don't believe it has to be this way.

Do I think we *can* avoid a slow, inexorable march toward an unrecognizable planet? Without a doubt. We can split the atom, we can peer into the structure of our own DNA, we can send satellites to bloody *Mars*. Our brains are—as far as we know—the most complex and sophisticated objects in the universe. Of course we can figure out how to live comfortably without making a horrible, stinky, cancerous mess everywhere. We already have every smidge of technology and know-how we need.

But do I think we *will* avoid catastrophe? Doubtful. Look at our track record. Look at what we spend our money, energy and hope on. Endless crap. Gargantuan McMansions we don't need (except to fill with more endless crap we don't need). Diamond-studded ass scratchers. And, of course, weapons. We spend more than a trillion dollars a year killing each other.

Humans can be artful, altruistic and sometimes rational, but there's no denying it: we are a race of greedy and selfish buggers sometimes. But I don't think that is any excuse for hedonism or despair. Humans are also endowed with at least one special gift: free will. Choice.

Choosing to be environmentally responsible isn't about squishy sentimentality—it's about intelligence. We need clean air, water and soil for our own sake. And it costs a lot more to clean up our mess than to prevent it in the first place. So we can choose not to be stupid. It's not rocket science, and it's not that difficult. Start with the easy stuff where you can (compost, take public transport, turn down the heat—you've heard this before). Stop buying stupid things you don't need (a no-brainer, whether you care about your bank balance or the planet). And most of all: vote, and pressure politicians. The richest of us can put up solar panels and buy organic cosmetics all we like, but only with legislation will we see true change on a meaningful scale.

With a critical mass of public support and legislative willpower, it really wouldn't be that hard to turn things around. Because our best estimates say it would take roughly $1 trillion—barely 1.6 percent of our global GDP last year, about what we spend annually on weapons—to cut carbon emissions by 50 percent (the minimum amount we need to prevent "catastrophic" climate change). If there's one thing we greedy humans love, it's a bargain. I've never heard of a better one. Let's hope we aren't too stupid to pass it up.

For Further Discussion

1. Walden Pond is often seen superficially as a pristine environment completely detached from the hustle and bustle of human endeavor. How is this depiction both true and untrue in *Walden*? (See Steinberg and Sattelmeyer.)

2. As a result of a misreading of *Walden*, Henry David Thoreau is often viewed as a hermit or an isolationist who wants no part of human affairs. How is Thoreau both deeply committed to the rest of humanity as well as to the natural environment? (See Myers.)

3. Thoreau is almost universally viewed as having been ahead of his time environmentally. Discuss Thoreau's continuing influence on modern environmentalism. (See Nash, Walls, McKibben, Nijhuis, and Agger.)

4. Is Thoreau more useful to contemporary followers as a spiritual guide (see McKibben) or as a practical one (see Nijhuis)?

5. A number of commentators have remarked on Thoreau's ambivalence toward nature and animals. Where does *Walden* display Thoreau's inconsistent attitudes about the natural environment? (See Morris and Bridgman.)

6. During his lifetime, Thoreau's attitude toward the environment marked him as an eccentric at best and a crazy man at worst. Even to this day, attitudes about the environment often tend toward extremes. Is it possible to take the middle ground and still be a committed environmentalist? (See Salam, Gingrich, Rothschild, Steel, and Cormier.)

For Further Reading

Edward Abbey, *Down the River*. New York: Dutton, 1982.

Edward Abbey, *The Monkey Wrench Gang*. Philadelphia: Lippincott, 1975.

Rachel Carson, Lois Darling, and Louis Darling, *Silent Spring*. Boston: Houghton Mifflin, 1962.

Annie Dillard, *Pilgrim at Tinker Creek*. New York: Harper's Magazine Press, 1974.

Jon Krakauer, *Into the Wild*. New York: Villard Books, 1996.

Aldo Leopold, *A Sand County Almanac, and Sketches Here and There*. New York: Oxford University Press, 1987.

Bill McKibben, *The Bill McKibben Reader: Pieces from an Active Life*. New York: Henry Holt, 2008.

John Muir, *Nature Writings: The Story of My Boyhood and Youth; My First Summer in the Sierra; the Mountains of California; Stickeen; Selected Essays*. New York: Library of America, 1997.

Henry David Thoreau, *Civil Disobedience and Other Essays*. New York: Dover Publications, 1993.

Henry David Thoreau, *The Natural History Essays*. Salt Lake City: Peregrine Smith, 1980.

Henry David Thoreau, *A Week on the Concord and Merrimac Rivers*. Boston: Houghton Mifflin, 1893.

Bibliography

Books

Greg Barton	*American Environmentalism.* San Diego, CA: Greenhaven Press, 2002.
Jane Bennett	*Thoreau's Nature: Ethics, Politics, and the Wild.* Thousand Oaks, CA: Sage Publications, 1994.
Michael P. Branch	*Reading the Roots: American Nature Writing Before Walden.* Athens: University of Georgia Press, 2004.
Joan Burbick	*Thoreau's Alternative History: Changing Perspectives on Nature, Culture, and Language.* Philadelphia: University of Pennsylvania Press, 1987.
Peter A. Fritzell	*Nature Writing and America: Essays upon a Cultural Type.* Ames: Iowa State University Press, 1990.
John Gatta	*Making Nature Sacred: Literature, Religion, and Environment in America from the Puritans to the Present.* New York: Oxford University Press, 2004.
Roger S. Gottlieb	*This Sacred Earth: Religion, Nature, Environment.* New York: Routledge, 1995.
Walter Roy Harding, ed.	*Thoreau: A Century of Criticism.* Dallas: Southern Methodist University Press, 1954.

Thomas Parke Hughes   *Changing Attitudes Toward American Technology.* New York: Harper & Row, 1975.

Lauriat Lane, ed.   *Approaches to Walden.* San Francisco: Wadsworth Pub. Co., 1961.

Michael L. Lewis   *American Wilderness: A New History.* Oxford and New York: Oxford University Press, 2007.

R.W.B. Lewis   *The American Adam: Innocence, Tragedy, and Tradition in the Nineteenth Century.* Chicago: University of Chicago Press, 1955.

Leo Marx   *The Machine in the Garden; Technology and the Pastoral Ideal in America.* New York: Oxford University Press, 1964.

F.O. Matthiessen   *American Renaissance: Art and Expression in the Age of Emerson and Whitman.* London and New York: Oxford University Press, 1941.

David Mazel   *American Literary Environmentalism.* Athens: University of Georgia Press, 2000.

Robert Kuhn McGregor   *A Wider View of the Universe: Henry Thoreau's Study of Nature.* Urbana: University of Illinois Press, 1997.

James McIntosh   *Thoreau as Romantic Naturalist: His Shifting Stance Toward Nature.* Ithaca: Cornell University Press, 1974.

James C.
McKusick

*Green Writing: Romanticism and
Ecology.* New York: St. Martin's Press,
2000.

Andrew McMurry

*Environmental Renaissance: Emerson,
Thoreau, and the System of Nature.*
Athens: University of Georgia Press,
2003.

Timothy Morton

*Ecology Without Nature: Rethinking
Environmental Aesthetics.* Cambridge,
MA: Harvard University Press, 2007.

Joel Myerson, ed.

*The Cambridge Companion to Henry
David Thoreau.* Cambridge and New
York: Cambridge University Press,
1995.

Joel Myerson, ed.

*Critical Essays on Henry David
Thoreau's Walden.* Boston: G.K. Hall,
1988.

Sherman Paul, ed.

*Thoreau: A Collection of Critical
Essays.* Englewood Cliffs, NJ:
Prentice-Hall, 1962.

Sandra Harbert
Petrulionis and
Laura Dassow
Walls

*More Day to Dawn: Thoreau's Walden
for the Twenty-first Century.* Amherst:
University of Massachusetts Press,
2007.

Donald Worster

*Nature's Economy: A History of
Ecological Ideas.* 2nd ed. Cambridge:
Cambridge University Press, 1995.

Periodicals

David Ackerson   "From Romanticism to Deep Ecology: The Continuing Evolution in American Environmental Thought," *Taproot*, vol. 12, no. 3, 2000.

John Bird   "Gauging the Value of Nature: Thoreau and His Woodchucks," *The Concord Saunterer*, vol. 2, 1994.

Daniel B. Botkin   "The Depth of Walden Pond: Thoreau as a Guide to Solving Twenty-first Century Environmental Problems," *The Concord Saunterer*, vol. 9, 2001.

Gerry Brenner   "Thoreau's 'Brute Neighbors': Four Levels of Nature," *Emerson Society Quarterly*, vol. 39, 1965.

Philip Cafaro   "Thoreau's Environmental Ethics in *Walden*," *The Concord Saunterer*, vol. 10, 2002.

George Cornell   "Native Americans and Environmental Thought: Thoreau and the Transcendentalists," *Akwe:Kon Journal*, vol. 9, no. 3, 1992.

Curriculum Review   "Teaching Students About the Environment with Henry David Thoreau," vol. 47, March 2008.

Stephen Fender   "The Environmental Imagination: *Walden* and Its Readers," *Journal of American Studies*, August 1997.

Walter Harding — "Five Ways of Looking at *Walden*," *Massachusetts Review*, Autumn 1962.

Koh Kasegawa — "Thoreau's *Walden*: A Nature-Myth," *Studies in English Literature*, November 1963.

Karl Kroeber — "Ecology and American Literature: Thoreau and Un-Thoreau," *American Literary History*, vol. 9, no. 2, 1997.

Lauriat Lane Jr. — "On the Organic Structure of *Walden*," *College English*, January 1960.

Melvin Lyon — "Walden Pond as Symbol," *PMLA*, May 1967.

William Rossi — "Education in the Field: Recent Thoreau Criticism and Environment," *ESQ: A Journal of the American Renaissance*, vol. 42, 1996.

Debra A. Segura — "'This Nature So Rife with Life': Ecological Consciousness in Walden," *AUMLA: Journal of the Australasian Universities Language and Literature Association*, vol. 102, 2004.

Index